CATS I'VE KNOWN

ON LOVE, LOSS, AND BEING GRACIOUSLY IGNORED

KATIE HAEGELE

MICROCOSM PUBLISHING
PORTLAND, OR

Cats I've Known

On Love, Loss, and Being Graciously Ignored

Katie Haegele

First published, October 10, 2017
© Katie Haegele, 2017
This edition is © by Microcosm Publishing, 2017
Cover and Illustrations by Trista Vercher, Vercher Ink

Microcosm Publishing
2752 N Williams Ave
Portland, OR 97227

For a catalog, write or visit
MicrocosmPublishing.com

ISBN 978-1-62106-481-7
This is Microcosm #272

Edited by Elly Blue
Designed by Joe Biel
Cover by Trista Vercher

Distributed worldwide by PGW and in Europe by Turnaround.

If you bought this on Amazon, I'm so sorry. You could have gotten it cheaper and supported a small, independent publisher at MicrocosmPublishing.com

The quote on page 17 is from *Lonesome Dove* by Larry McMurtry

Library of Congress Cataloging-in-Publication Data

Names: Haegele, Katie, author

Title: Cats I've known / Katie Haegele.

Description: First edition. | Portland, OR : Microcosm Publishing, 2017.

   Identifiers: LCCN 2016048193 (print) | LCCN 2017024118 (ebook) | ISBN
   9781621060123 (epdf) | ISBN 9781621061274 (epub) | ISBN 9781621064855 (
   mobi/kindle) | ISBN 9781621064817 (pbk.)

Subjects: LCSH: Cats--Anecdotes. | Haegele, Katie.

Classification: LCC SF445.5 (ebook) | LCC SF445.5 .H34 2017 (print) | DDC
   636.8--dc23

LC record available at https://lccn.loc.gov/2016048193

MICROCOSM · PUBLISHING

Microcosm Publishing is Portland's most diversified publishing house and distributor with a focus on the colorful, authentic, and empowering. Our books and zines have put your power in your hands since 1996, equipping readers to make positive changes in their lives and in the world around them. Microcosm emphasizes skill-building, showing hidden histories, and fostering creativity through challenging conventional publishing wisdom with books and bookettes about DIY skills, food, bicycling, gender, self-care, and social justice. What was once a distro and record label was started by Joe Biel in his bedroom and has become among the oldest independent publishing houses in Portland, OR. We are a politically moderate, centrist publisher in a world that has inched to the right for the past 80 years.

Global labor conditions are bad, and our roots in industrial Cleveland in the 70s and 80s made us appreciate the need to treat workers right. Therefore, our books are MADE IN THE USA and printed on post-consumer paper.

TABLE OF CONTENTS

INTRODUCTION

THE BACKYARD
SAGA BEGINS

I can see them from here: The mama cat and her litter of two kittens romping around in our backyard. The mother is lounging on her side, watching as her daffy babies tumble over each other and roll around in the grass. She's black with a white belly and the babies are both the same dark grey color and covered in fuzz.

I'm having my morning coffee at my kitchen table, which sits under two huge windows that look out onto the narrow backyard of my Philadelphia row house. It's my favorite place in this whole house to sit and work—like I am right now—or to talk to my mom on the phone, or to drink a beer while our little radio plays 107.9, Philly's new throwback hip-hop station, which is easily the best one in town.

From my spot at the table I can see our whole yard, as well as the entirety of both yards on either side, plus the row of houses behind ours and the busy street at the bottom of it. Out front, the door to our house opens right onto the sidewalk; we don't even have a real stoop. When people walk down our street I can see their faces from my living room, and on a warm day when the windows are open, I can hear every word they say. I grew up in a suburb just outside this city, where there was a bit more space and it was a bit more quiet. But I've always wanted to live in a house like this one, all tucked in with my neighbors snug on either side and signs of life all around me. When Joe and I got married and agreed to move to the city, this is the neighborhood I chose, and it's perfect. There's trash on the sidewalks and some shady people who hang out around the bus stop, but there's a lot of beauty here, too.

And it's been funny, getting used to having these stray cats around. I've had lots of pet cats in my life, but these aren't anybody's pets. They're not exactly wild, though, either—they need us people, and our garbage, and the occasional moments of kindness we have to offer. Joe and I keep an eye on them but we haven't needed to worry about them much; we've been here for nearly a year now and we still haven't had a cold spell. It's December, but it's been unseasonably warm since the summer ended, which I guess is why the mama and her babies are looking so relaxed out there. They've got a long, yellow strip of sun to loll around in, and the grass hasn't even died.

We see the same strays again and again and have enjoyed getting to know them from a distance, like neighbors who you wave to when you see them but basically don't know. The mama cat uses our backyard as a hangout and a through-way and there's something delightful about spotting her back there. She's a tough old thing with a slight limp and a wonky eye, features we interpreted—entirely uncritical of the gender essentializing we were engaging in—to mean that she was a he. "The old guy," we called the cat whenever we saw it. "Hey look, the old guy is on the shed again. He's staring at us!" one of us would say. A few times we saw the cat on the wooden bench in our backyard or sitting on the roof of that tin shed next door, but more often than that it's in transit, rarely at ease, never resting or sleeping for long. That's the life of a stray, I guess.

And anyway, he turned out to be a she, which we knew because she had kittens, which we found out one morning at breakfast when Joe saw her come trotting through the yard with a tiny, dark baby swinging from her mouth. We watched, eyes huge, as she and her cargo squirmed under the fence to our neighbor Frank's yard, then hid herself and her kitten under a dirty old plastic bin that was propped against one of the tires he keeps back there.

Frank is an older guy who has lived here forever and he's pretty eccentric. You could call him one of the drawbacks to living here, I guess, but actually he's alright. He owns the house next to ours, a small parking lot next to that, and the house on the other side of the lot, and all three of these properties are filled with mysterious hulking objects that are covered in tarps and other makeshift structures. The tiny walkway between our house and his is also jammed full of junk— -buckets, upturned rakes, snarls of rope or hose or something like that—and he owns four rusted-out jalopies: a truck and three ancient cars that he keeps on the street in front of his houses at all times so that no one else can park near him. It's hard to say what exactly Frank has going on over there, and I can't help but feel curious. The man who rents our house to us grew up in this neighborhood and he told us that when he was young, Frank apprenticed with the last remaining goldsmith in the city. Together they repaired the massive chandeliers that hang—or used to hang—from the ceilings of the fancy department stores downtown. A lot of the junk Frank collects in his yards looks like it's made of metal, so I guess he might be using his smithing skills to make something, maybe art of some kind. But I doubt it. The whole arrangement seems odder and sadder than that. And since Frank rarely does more than nod hello, I'm not sure if we'll ever find out.

But as I was saying, or meant to say, this morning is shaping up to be a nice one. I'm sitting in my sunny kitchen on a day in early winter, watching the cat watch her kittens play. It's lovely, and it feels like a blessing, too, since the reason I sat down here in the first place was to begin writing this book about cats. It's an auspicious beginning, I think.

I should let you know that I have changed the names of some of the people in these stories, but the details are true to how I remember them, except for the ones that are not my memories but are stories that were told to me by people I know. I want to thank them for the use of those tales and ask them to forgive me for any poetic license I took in bringing them to life. And thank you, readers, for being here and listening to me tell stories about these cats who have all meant so much to me. I hope you'll get a kick out of them, too.

1

OPHELIA

phelia was beautiful and aloof, and the first cat I ever knew. She was my mother's cat, and the cat never liked anyone but her.

My mom got Ophelia when she was sixteen, which is why she gave her that fanciful name: They were reading *Hamlet* in school. Her neighbor's cat had kittens and she was invited over to choose one. The girl who would become my mother peered down into a cardboard box in her neighbor's garage and all but one of the kittens scrambled around, trying to get her attention. The one she liked best was pure white, with bright green eyes, and that one sat away from the others in a corner and paid no attention to my mother at all.

"I like a cat that has *personality*," my mom explained—her preferred personality, I guess, being grouchy.

Still, the cat had gumption. After high school, but before she got married, when my mother still lived with her parents in the old neighborhood, she had a bedroom on the third floor. She liked to sit in the window seat up there and read, and her cat, when she could manage it, liked to sneak out the open window and tiptoe around the eaves of the roof, three stories up, thirty feet in the air, like a tightrope walker.

Ophelia had a partner-in-crime in that house, too—Tuesday the dog. The cat would jump up to the shelf in the pantry where the dog food was kept and knock the bag over so that it spilled out onto the floor, where the dog was waiting to gobble it up. I don't know if the dog ever did anything for the cat in return.

Ophelia lived to be nineteen; pretty old for a cat. Long enough for my mother to finish high school and go on countless dreary Friday night dates with boys from the neighborhood, start working in an office downtown, meet my dad there, get married, leave the cat with my grandparents when her new husband got a job in one foreign country, then another, return home a few years later, have a baby, then a second one. I was six when her beloved old cat died and was unable to imagine my mother existing before I did, but when it happened that's what she grieved for, all those years and things she'd lived through with her constant, quiet companion as a witness. With the cat gone there was no longer a through line from that time to the present, and her past lifted up into the air and disappeared with nothing to anchor it.

SYLVESTER

ylvester was our family cat when I was growing up, but he wasn't much of a pet. He didn't care for cuddling and he preferred to be outdoors, killing birds and terrorizing the neighbors' cats. We could hear them fighting a block away, their long screams like wild banshee cries in the night. He was one badass tuxedo on the prowl.

When he was little, my parents took Sylvester to the vet to be neutered. The doctor put him under the anesthesia and attempted to perform the very routine surgery, but couldn't; mysteriously, though his anatomy looked normal from the outside, there was nothing there. My parents liked to joke that Sly, as they called him, was hiding his stuff from the doctors so that he could keep it. That's how big of a boss he was.

In keeping with his tough-guy persona, Sylvester liked to watch boxing on TV. It was the only thing he ever took notice of on the screen. When my dad put on a match, the cat would come sit on his knee and watch the fighters, rapt, his eyes flitting back and forth and his tail waving like a flag.

When, many years later, we found poor Sylvester dead of old age near the basement steps out back, we barely noticed. It happened about a month after my father died, during the hottest summer we'd had in years, and the three of us remaining humans—my mom, my sister, and I—were just too tired. We didn't have any sadness leftover for old Sly. But that seems fitting, now that I think about it. He died alone like the cowboy he was, and didn't need anybody to mark it. If a bullet had taken him down he would have taken a glug of whiskey and pulled it out with his teeth, saying, *Yesterday's gone on down the river and you can't get it back.*

3

THE WHITE CAT "STATUE"

hen I was growing up, my grandmother's house had this ornament in it: A white plastic cat about eighteen inches tall that sat on the living room floor. It must have been a bottle that held, like, bubble bath or something, because its head screwed off at the neck. The cat's face had that retro 60s look, with shapely eyes like a woman's made-up with black eyeliner, and they were a garish green that looked so beautiful to me. When I was a kid, every time we went to visit, my grandmother would play *hide the cat head* with me and we'd take turns hiding it around the house for the other to find.

I wonder now if my grandmother kept that bottle because she liked it or because she thought my sister and I would. Grandmom Cookie, as we called her, had tons of cool stuff in her house. She always had cookies, hence the nickname. She also had a wooden box that was a cigarette holder for loosies hanging on her kitchen wall that said COFFIN NAILS on it. She had *piles* of secondhand jewelry—painted metal flower brooches and plastic clip-on earrings—in jewelry boxes with drawers. She even had her own shopping cart thing with wheels, and because she never learned to drive, she'd push her cart to the bus that would take her to the supermarket and back. Her house was smaller than ours and it was jam-packed full of her things, which gave the rooms a cozy, muffled feeling—and yet it was tidy and so ferociously clean you could have performed surgery on the arm of the couch.

There was plenty of . . . less cool stuff in that house, too. Poor Grandmom Cookie was a little loony about her Catholicism. She'd been raised in the church, but was forced out of it when she married a Jew. Back then, marrying anyone who wasn't a Catholic was enough to get you kicked out of the club, and she either didn't mind this or coped with it well for a while, but then got very weird. The most obvious expression of this weirdness was the amazing amount of lurid Catholic paraphernalia she'd festooned her small house with. And the worst example of *that* was her copy of the *Pietà*. You know Michelangelo's *Pietà*, the sculpture of Mary holding the body of Jesus after the crucifixion? That was done in white marble? Well, my grandmother had one, in plaster, in *color*. The colors were bright and there was a lot of *red*. For *blood*. You could see the statue when you climbed the stairs to the second floor, where it seemed to peer out of the dimness of a quiet, disused bedroom. You had to run as fast as you could to get around the corner and away from it every time you went up to use the bathroom.

But the white cat statue, that was really nice. At a thrift store a few years ago, Joe and I found a black cat statue, a shiny, painted, ceramic one that was about the same size and style as the one I remember from Grandmom's house, sitting pretty, slender, and elongated, tail wrapped around the feet. I bought it, of course, and it sits on our bedroom floor now, next to our bookcase, reminding me of *hide the cat head* and other sweet things.

4

SISTER EUSTACE & THE LIBRARY CAT

ister Eustace was evil, like all the other nuns who taught me in school. She wasn't a teacher, though—she was a librarian, the steward of our small but surprisingly complete school library, with its hard-woven industrial carpeting and crispy, brown houseplants. This was back in the Dark Ages, when you used the library the old-fashioned way: With a card catalog that was a piece of furniture filled with actual cards. We had computers too, but you couldn't do research that way; not yet. Maybe somebody knew how to, but all we used them for was typing simple lines of code in Fortran, which, like magic, could spit back the answers to your math homework. Things were so different back then. The internet wasn't everywhere, invisible in the air around you; it lived in our uninspiring computer lab and got locked up in there at night. When you had a report to do, you went to Sister's library and used the books you found there, unless your paper was more challenging and you had to make use of the public library instead. It didn't occur to us to do it any other way because there wasn't any other way to do it.

So yeah, the library was Sister Eustace's domain, and though she threatened to throw us out for giggling during every study hall we spent there, she wasn't much for shows of anger. She was just sour, in a not-especially-nun-like way. She could have been any other ground-down, middle-aged person who detested youth and beauty or whatever; whatever it is that's wrong with all the mean people who are put in charge of kids.

The only semisweet thing Sister Eustace ever did was make a fuss over Pet Week, which now that I think about it must have been something she made up. Students were encouraged to bring in photos of their families' cats and dogs (and, more rarely, birds and snakes and fish) and tack them to the bulletin board; the same board that my best friend Maura and I once defaced by changing around the letters in GOING ON THIS WEEK to GOING ON SHIT WEEK.

Sister loved cats above all other animals and she had a cat of her own. She brought it into the library as often as she could get away with and it could usually be found there all throughout Pet Week. It really was a treat to see an animal at school. Her cat had the seal-point coloring of a Siamese, but it was round and luxurious rather than angular and bony. When you took your book up to the desk to be checked out, there the cat would be, curled up fat and sleek on the counter looking disdainful and self-satisfied, like any cat that's worth a damn.

The thing that makes this story noteworthy is how completely unusual it was for a nun to have a pet, or really anything that cost money and made a display of any sort of individuality. That's the thing about being a nun: They receive no salary, having taken a vow of poverty, and they live together in communities and dress alike. Individuality is more of a worldly thing, you know? But Sister had somehow snagged this sweet deal for herself. The nuns who taught at the school all lived across the street in the convent house, which was on a rather large property for the modest city neighborhood it was in. But instead of living in the main house with the other evil nuns, Sister Eustace lived alone in a cottage on the property. And she had a cat, like any other single lady you might know. I have no idea how it was that she had such an arrangement, but as you know, in school every tiny personal detail about the teachers gets scooped up greedily and shared widely, so we all knew about Sister Eustace's bachelorette pad. I still think about that sometimes, about Sister's secrets, and the private lives of nuns in general, and the ways that women have found, across generations, to get a piece of independence wherever they could grab it.

I stroked her cat's fur once and it bit me.

LOCUST
MOON

Locust Moon is closed now, but it was everybody's favorite West Philly comic book store for a few years. The store was always dimly lit and cozy, and they had this beautiful aquarium set into the wall with a picture frame around it, so it looked like an animated painting.

It had a magical energy, like all the best bookstores do. When you walked in, one of their two cats was likely to greet you or ignore you or some tantalizing combination of the two. Rooster was a scruffy ragamuffin whose fur was longer on his tail than on the rest of his body so he looked like a squirrel. Inky was the bigger, badder of the two. He'd nudge your hand roughly with his big, old head to let you know you should pat him, then pop his behind up in the air so you'd be sure to get his back, too.

One time I went in there to pick up some books the owners had donated to a fundraising effort I was helping to organize. I felt shy, as I always do when I enter a mostly-masculine space, especially when I have to announce my presence in some way. The awkwardness levels can climb dangerously high.

Sure enough, the only folks who were there that day were guys—the two owners and a young teenager who I got the feeling spent a lot of time there after school. They were all hanging out by the front counter—including Inky, who was standing in front of the register. I made a fuss over the cat and we all took a moment to admire his I-don't-give-a-crap-itude. He liked my attention, but gave the impression that he could take it or leave it: The hallmark of the cool cat.

I wanted to ask about the books, but I could feel my face burning with the old embarrassment that to this day rises up in me whenever I'm the only woman in a group of men. It must be the lifelong legacy of going to all-girls schools. But then the kid, who'd been standing beside me, said with surprising passion, "I wish I was a cat," and I knew I was among friends.

"Me too!" I said, and hopped around in a little dance of dorky excitement. "I've always said that!" Like, I really have always said that it would be awesome to be a cat. Total superhero status: You'd be nocturnal and elegant, with superior eyesight and a set of mean blades at the end of each foot. Me and the kid agreed that it would be baller to slip around town at night—to own the city and all its invisible hideouts like one of the dark fighters of crime. You know, like Batman. Catman. Catwoman!

I still smile when I remember this conversation, a rare moment of connection between me and a nerdy teenage boy, two people who would most likely have remained terrified of each other if it wasn't for Inky bringing folks together.

6

SYLVIA

ylvia was a cruel little creature. Beautiful, but cruel. She was my mother's cat, even though she adopted her when my dad was still alive and Liz and I were still in high school—an intact family. I guess she wanted a cat of her own, and left to her own devices she picked the kind of cat no one else in the family would have chosen: A tiny, perfect, pedigreed one that no one could get near without being skinned alive.

Sylvia was a purebred Persian cat, with papers and everything. My mother bought her from two kooky breeders, a couple who lived in a Philadelphia suburb a few miles from ours. She got to choose the kitten she wanted from a litter that had been born several weeks earlier by going to the ladies' messy house to meet and play with them all. She must have been in heaven.

Sylvia looked like an adorable insect, with a flat face and huge round eyes. Her long, thick fur was like a rainbow, if rainbows were made up entirely of every shade of the color grey. The day my mother brought her home she ran and hid under my parents' bed, and there she remained for the rest of her life. Not under the bed, but on it. For the better part of the day, every day, for the following twenty years, she sat curled up on that bed, surrounded by pillows like a sultan. Walking past the room, it was tempting to stop in there and try to touch the cat's silky fur, but you did so at your own risk. Lots of cats are mean because they're fearful, and they only swipe at you because they don't want to be touched. They have boundaries. I can respect that. The unusual, and frankly ridiculous, thing about Sylvia's meanness was that it was petty. She could hold a grudge. If you stroked her fur for too long, say, or sat down too close to her on the bed where she was installed, she'd get mad at you, and she'd stay mad. She'd remember your transgression and then, some time later—once you'd moved to the foot of the bed and forgotten about her—she'd run at you from behind and give you a smack. You know that THUMP that cats can give you? Even when they don't use their claws, it hurts! Every time she did that I thought of the mice she'd killed, tiny huntress that she was, and tried to imagine what a whack like that would feel like if you only weighed half an ounce.

My father enjoyed teasing my mother for her devotion to the little monster and her habit of calling the cat "my darling Sylvia." And now that I think about it, Sylvia wasn't mean to him. He was one of the few people who was allowed to pick her up in his arms, and he'd do so fairly often, carrying her around like a baby, stroking her head, and cooing to her—pretending he was kidding around, but totally not. His mood could be as prickly as the cat's; I guess they understood each other. Poor Dad.

Sylvia's fur tended to get tangled and matted, so it had to be cut fairly often. If you have any acquaintance with Persian or other long-haired cats, you may be familiar with the lion cut. If not, go ahead and Google it. It's an endearingly unattractive look. A few times a year, my mother would take Sylvia to a groomer's to have her entire body shaved down, except for her tufty, bearded head—which then resembled a lion's mane—and the tip of her tail—which came out looking like a mace. A soft, fluffy mace. I don't know, I Googled "lion cut" just now and those pictures don't quite reach the same levels of ugliness that Sylvia's haircut always did. She was unusually tiny, with delicate, prominent bones, and the buzzcut made her look like a squirrel—a pitiful squirrel, like one that had forgotten where its acorns were buried. Poor Sylvie.

Sylvia died a few months ago of good, old-fashioned old age. I know my mom is still feeling down about it. Nineteen years is a long time to be friends with somebody, and the death of a beloved pet is an unhappy reminder of the fate that's in store for all of us, even if we, like Sylvia, are lucky enough to live a long and healthy life.

Poor everybody.

I fucking love this cat. She has such an attitude, it's amazing. Domineering, demanding, and capricious, Gloria will bear down on you and insist on sitting on your lap—or your hip, or your shoulder—whether you like it or not. Unless she doesn't feel like company, that is, in which case she'll stick her ass up in the air and walk away.

Gloria is my sister's cat, the A1, first-ever cat in what is now a five-cat household, if you don't count the outdoor cats she and her boyfriend have also taken to feeding. As the oldest and first, Gloria plays the part of the *grande dame*, queening it up around the other cats with their simpleton antics. But the truth is she's been a Queen Bee since she was a tiny kitten who tried to make a nest in my hair.

Gloria is named for the Patti Smith song. "G-L-O-R-I-A!" Patti Smith is one of my sister's all-time sheroes, and despite Liz's supposed hatred of "hipsters," she ate up every word of that memoir Smith wrote about living with Robert Mapplethorpe at the Chelsea Hotel. I mean, come on. I must say though, Gloria is a good name for a punk-attitude cat like her. "People say beware, but I don't care. / The words are just rules and regulations to me."

When Liz adopted Gloria, she was living in an apartment with a friend she worked with at H&M, and the three of them formed an oddball family of sorts. I remember being surprised that Liz got a cat because she'd teased me so mercilessly about my cat-lady ways, but her devotion to this small, spotted fur ball she brought home from the pound was immediate and total.

Gloria is one of those cats with fur that's so plush she feels like a rabbit, and all these years later she's still as soft as she was when she was a kitten. Back when she actually was a kitten, she kept me awake one night after Liz and I came home from some party. I crashed at her apartment and we shared the bed, and Liz's adorable new kitten spent the entire night being extremely interested in kneading my scalp as though my head was one big mama cat's belly. Ever so gently with her tiny needle claws—*poke poke poke poke poke*—and I never woke up properly, just enough to try to shoo her away. Going out with Liz like that was unusual enough—I think I only stayed over at her place one other time—so it's a nice memory, even though I felt wrecked the next day.

Gloria has seen Liz through several phases of her life, from that first apartment to a handful of others and a career change that took her out of offices and into gardens. Now the two of them—plus a few others she picked up along the way—live in a house she shares with a sweet guy named Marty. Marty has his own cat, Boris, though Boris came into Marty's life because of my sister, too, to tell the truth. But that's a story for another time.

For several years before I got married, I lived alone in an apartment in a small, red, brick building. Well, I wasn't really alone—I lived with my best pal, Trixie, a sleek, black cat. I'll tell you more about her soon.

Behind the brick building was a tiny, adorable dollhouse of a cottage. It used to be the carriage house of the larger property next to it and a lady lived there with her cat and her sweet little boy. The kid had autism and he sometimes played with the older kids on the block, but with some difficulty. I could hear them yelling back there sometimes, and his voice had a strange note in it; you knew without looking that something was different about him.

The woman, Lydia, she was interesting, too. You could tell she'd lived a little. Up close, her tattoos showed from underneath her black ballet tops, and once Joe and I saw her boyfriend take off early in the morning on a motorcycle. She had rock star status in our minds after that.

But the salient detail about all this was Max. Max was Lydia's huge, dark grey, long-haired cat who liked to prowl around the driveway behind my building. He was beautiful and impressive, but comical, too. He acted like a tough guy, but he'd roll onto his back after just a moment if you paid him any attention at all. Sometimes I'd encounter him not in the driveway but on the sidewalk as I made my way down the street. On those occasions, if I was headed home, Max would hop up onto the old, stone wall that ringed my building and trot along beside me, letting out yowling sounds as he went. When he got to a break in the wall where there was a walk leading up to one of the doors, he'd always pause, and I'd feel this crazy longing for him to make the jump and continue following me. He almost always did. Being followed by Max felt like a victory, as if I had a magical cat friend who'd sometimes appear to keep me company, like in a Nintendo game.

Once he got to know me better, Max got bolder, and he'd try to get inside my building as I unlocked the front door. A few times he succeeded, and then got tangled in my legs as I walked up the stairs. I'd get cross and nudge him back out the door and he'd hang around the front step for a while after that, looking desolate. Every time I'd take a peek, he'd still be there, looking up into my eyes through the window, penetratingly, willing me to open the door again and let him in. Through the thick glass I could see his mouth open, but I couldn't hear his cries.

It turned out Max was a lot of people's special friend. One time Joe and I saw Lydia on our way out somewhere and we stopped to tell her how much we liked Max.

"He's so funny and friendly!" I said. "He walks right up to us."

"Oh yeah, he likes everybody," Lydia said agreeably. Apparently, in her old neighborhood he'd go into people's houses the way he'd followed me into mine, but they'd let him stay, feeding him dinner and fussing over him, so that later in the evening, when he turned up missing, Lydia had to make the rounds, eventually tracking him to a warm living room where he was curled up on the couch with somebody's kids, watching TV.

We saved Max's life once, or so I like to think. One Saturday evening in early summer, while it was still light out, Joe and I returned home to my place after being out all day. I had on tight jeans that were cuffed high on the ankle and the kind of comfy sandals that slip on easily and slap on the ground as you walk. We parked the car across the street and had just taken our bags out of the car when a cat came bounding down the driveway toward us.

"Hi buddy!" Joe called, thinking it was Max or another friendly neighborhood cat, when we saw to our horror that it was not a cat at all, but a big, rabid raccoon that was bobbing its head around like an old drunk as it ran right at us. I yelled Joe's name, more dismayed than panicked because I knew I couldn't run fast enough in my stupid shoes to get away in time. In my mind, I saw those long claws dragging nasty slashes down my tender, exposed skin. Joe had just enough time to position himself to take aim, then hurl the twenty-pound bag of potting soil he was holding, which nailed the raccoon in the chest. It stopped, staggered backward, then loped off in a different direction just as blindly as it had come at us, like a wind-up toy that got picked up and plunked down somewhere else.

Amid a flurry of *holy shit!* and *did you see that?* we remembered Max, who was almost always outdoors. We had to warn Lydia! We ran to her door and knocked, out of breath like two little kids. When she answered she was on the phone, weary but polite. "Oh! I'll go look for the cat, yeah," she said, and we could tell she didn't quite believe us. No one quite believed this story when we told it to people later, or at least they didn't respond with the appropriate amount of alarm. But we were glad we'd warned Lydia, and we called the police too, since there was totally a scary, wild animal on the loose. And sure enough, in the local paper that week, I read that a girl had been bitten by a rabid raccoon that same evening, and that the animal was found dead the next morning in someone's backyard.

Lydia, her son, and the cat moved away several months later and my walks through the neighborhood were emptier without Max. I wonder if he's still a charmer, wherever he is, breaking hearts and hogging couches in his new town.

THE TRUTH IS OUT THERE

Imagine it's the late nineties and you're a fun-loving young woman who lives with her best friend in an apartment downtown. You've just graduated from college but your roommate Johanna finished the year before, and she adopted a cat before you moved in together. And since Johanna is a massive *X-Files* fan, that cat's name is Mulder.

You and Johanna have a ton of fun together. You watch *Felicity* and scream at the embarrassing parts, and there's a Spice Girls poster on your bathroom wall. Johanna's a smart, funny person, and the first serious fan you've ever known. An early adopter of internet culture, she spends hours on the computer in conversation with strangers about *Buffy* and her other favorite shows. She makes you go to see the *X-Files* movie with her when it comes out, and you don't hate it. And when she buys the collectible Mulder and Scully figures they put out to promote the movie, the two of you sprawl out on the living room floor and act out all the dialogue you can remember.

Over all this foolishness, Mulder (the cat) looks on. He is a large, striped, grey tabby who is extremely chill and kind of wimpy. He makes an incongruously tiny *mew* sound, when he makes any sound at all.

When Johanna decided she wanted to get a cat, she'd checked Craigslist, where she saw an ad for the one remaining cat from a litter that had been born in the backyard of a family in North Jersey. The cat was already big, the lady warned her. And he was! For a kitten he was huge, and he would only get bigger. Now, if you're not from New Jersey or somewhere close to it, you probably don't know about Jersey feral cats. Growing up in Philadelphia, we all knew that the feral cats in New Jersey were bigger than feral cats anywhere else—pumas, practically—and though this could have been an urban legend, Mulder's presence in our lives seemed to confirm it as fact. He had big, awkward feet and a long, strong tail like a whip. We believed that this was because he had some quasi-mystical feral provenance— descended from lynxes, we'd always heard—and the idea gave us a thrill. Whatever his background, he really was a fine looking cat. He swung his hips out as he sauntered around, knowing how good he looked. Johanna called it his supermodel swagger.

The year I lived with Johanna was the year my father died, and after that happened I packed up my things and moved back home with my mom. Things between my old roomie and I were strained after that, though I can't say I completely understand why. I think I just didn't want to bring anything of my old, light-hearted life into my new, sadder one; my barely-grown-up friends, even the kindest ones, like Johanna, were too immature to live in the Land of Grief with me for as long as I needed their company there. She and I haven't seen each for a long time now, but I miss her loony sense of humor and matter-of-fact profanity, the way she could be counted on to call the TV show "Growing Pains" *Groin Pains* instead, and her reworked tagline from the cosmetics ads: "Easy, sleazy, cheesy—Cover Girl." I think of her sometimes and wonder how she and Mulder are getting on.

20

THE WANNABE

I had another cat friend in my old neighborhood besides Max: The Wannabe.

The Wannabe was a little, black cat that I'd see on my way through the streets, making my usual rounds to the post office or the library. The cat was always on the same block, though it didn't seem to be anybody's pet. Something about the way it slipped around, silent and sleek, keen to avoid people but never really afraid—I could tell it was on its own. I called it The Wannabe because it was shiny and black like my cat, Trixie, and since Trixie reigned supreme over all black cats, any other must be a wannabe, right? She was the coolest of them all.

Still, The Wannabe possessed a fair amount of inner chill. It let me stroke its fur sometimes, but after a moment it would lose interest, stand up abruptly, and walk away, as if to say, "*That'll do.*" It didn't get mean and it wasn't scared. It was just cool as a cucumber with someplace to be.

I loved coming across The Wannabe on my walks. It was such an elegant cat and it seemed to complete every scene it was in. I'd catch it picking its way through someone's messy garden of wildflowers, or sitting on the church steps, or sleeping in the sun on a low, stone wall, and it appeared almost indistinct from its surroundings, part of the landscape somehow.

One winter it snowed so much, so many times, that we had nearly three feet of snow on the ground for some time, and after a while the piles of snow were encased in a shiny layer of ice. Eventually shoveling became such a nuisance that most people didn't bother anymore, but the ones who attempted it created a kind of tunnel down the sidewalk, a narrow pathway with walls of snow on either side that were nearly as tall as me. It was magical walking through these tunnels. There wasn't room for two people to pass each other, so you always got the tunnel to yourself, and the world went quiet and white and chill for a moment, like a Björk video or something.

My mom, who lived nearby, had seen The Wannabe and liked it as much as I did. On her way home from church one evening, she spotted the cat sitting and posing at the end of a snow tunnel. She made her way down the sidewalk and toward it, a black silhouette in the bluish twilight, but it walked away before she could reach it, and when it stepped behind the wall of snow it seemed to disappear.

THE BACKYARD SAGA CONTINUES

I t was a strange thing, having kittens in a weirdly mild early winter like the one we had through the end of the year. Day after day, the Mama cat and her two kittens could be seen lazing and romping and streaking through our backyard. I wondered to myself whether cats weren't supposed to have their kittens in the spring instead, but figured they must have been okay because the weather was so warm. Deep into December the sun was out, the air was mild, the breeze was soft. But then the winter solstice came, and the new year, and then yesterday—finally—it got cold. It was windy as fuck, too. I had to wait a while at the train station around the corner and it doesn't have a shelter to hide in, so the other riders and I stood on the platform with tears running down our faces.

During the night we got a light dusting of snow and it was bitter this morning when Joe left for work. After I said goodbye to him at the door, I shuffled around putting things away and got on the phone with my mom—my usual procrastination routine before I sit down to start my day of writing and other work. As I walked through the kitchen and passed the big window that overlooks the yard, I saw one of the tiny kittens alone—fuzzy and clueless as ever—padding unsteadily over a crunchy layer of snow. I was still on the phone when I saw it.

"Mom! The kitten! It's one of the kittens!" I couldn't believe it. Why was it on its own? I opened the back door, which is a noisy ordeal since it's old and it sticks and you first have to slam your rear-end against it to close it enough for the bolt to slide across.

Then the second lock, the deadbolt, snaps open like a shot. The kitten took off when it heard me, scrambling desperately, and I was almost able to grab it as it darted toward the fence between our yard and Frank's. But it was too quick, and tiny enough to squeeze through a hole in the chain link. The poor thing thought it was trapped once it was over there and kept running back and forth between the two walls of Frank's back porch. Finally, it found its way through and disappeared into his shantytown of confusing tarp structures.

I stayed on the phone with my mother throughout all this silliness and we talked about how I could lure the kitten back to my yard. She agreed it wouldn't hurt to set out some food, even though Joe is strictly against feeding the strays. What he doesn't know won't hurt him. I opened a can of tuna and put a tiny amount in a tea cup, then went out back and set the cup on one of the wooden planks around our raised garden bed, several feet from the house so the kitten wouldn't feel afraid to approach. Back inside, I was practically wringing my hands with anxiety, worrying about the baby cat being on its own in this cold. I kept peering out the window until I saw the kitten eating greedily from the cup—with its mother just beside it. Phew. Still, the little one was trembling; I could see so from inside. If I couldn't catch it, I thought, maybe I could make a house for them both to warm up in.

We didn't have much in the way of materials, so I took an old cardboard box and taped black trash bags to the bottom, then cut a door into the side and put a blanket inside it. According to the internet, none of this is adequate. Cardboard doesn't do much to insulate against the cold and blankets make bad bedding because they'll get wet. It seems the best type of cat shelter is one made out of a Styrofoam ice chest with a tiny hole cut in the bottom for drainage and straw for bedding. That could be my next project, then. For now, the box would do. I set it under the choke cherry tree, which had protected the ground underneath it from snow.

From my lookout seat at the kitchen table, the Mama and baby look pretty happy right now. They're playing in the thick pachysandra that grows at the back of the yard, where it's sunniest: I can sometimes see the flickering movement of tiny white paws through the growth. Every so often one of them makes a skirmish to the cup of food. The kitten's tail is tiny and comes to a point and fuzz stands out over its whole coat, like a black dandelion. It looks so vulnerable out there. I hope they'll decide to spend the night in the little hut I made. I don't know what happened to the other kitten and I've decided not to think too much about that. I'll see what we can do for the one that's still here and hope for the best for the others in the neighborhood.

12

TRIXIE

When I was twenty-one, I got a cat of my own.

I was working at a university, on a campus that was right next to the college I'd just graduated from. My walk to work was almost the same as the walk I'd made to class the year before, on the street that formed a bridge over the river that flowed through the middle of the city. I shared an apartment downtown with my best friend and her cat. My job was as a writer for an in-house publishing group that made promotional materials for the university. It meant a lot to me to find work as a writer, in large part because it meant a lot to my dad, who had hounded me to get a job until I found this one. I had my own desk, but most days I worked with Barry, a long-suffering graphic designer with gorgeous, black, Mark Almond hair who'd gone to art school in the 80s and still had a tiny, gold hoop in one ear. I often spent the entire day perched right next to him as he clicked and moved words I'd written around on his special widescreen monitor.

"I spend more time with you than I do with my wife, Katie," he once said, the note in his voice incredulous but not unkind. All in all it was an okay job.

I worked in the dean's office and next door to us was admissions. I got to know some of those folks eventually, usually by bumping into them in the big marble hallway or sitting out front on the big marble steps, smoking a cigarette and sometimes crying because my dad was sick and was probably going to die. One of the people I met from admissions, Jim, stood out from the other employees in that office because he was old and a man, and he was small and seemed solitary and sad. My boss introduced me to him and later she told me he'd been a Catholic priest.

Jim and I would hang out by the copy machine, neither of us in a big hurry to get back to work. I told him about my apartment and he told me about his cat, who would sit behind his head on the couch while he watched movies on TV.

"What's your cat's name?" I asked.

"He doesn't have a name," Jim said. He made the smallest, saddest smile, but it was still a smile. "He's just a little black cat."

After I'd been out of school and working for a few months, I decided I wanted a cat too. Every young single woman I knew who lived in an apartment in the city had a pet cat and I was starting to feel left out. And although I did love Mulder, I wanted a cat that would be my own special friend. I fancied the idea of a black one—"just a little black cat"—most of all.

I called the office of a vet that wasn't too long a walk from my apartment and asked whether they knew of any cats that needed homes. I see now that this was an odd way to go about it, but I'd never adopted a cat before, so I didn't know what you were supposed to do. And anyway, it worked.

"Actually, we do. Well, *I* do," said the vet tech who answered the phone. She told me that several weeks earlier a young black cat had appeared on her porch on Halloween. She'd asked around and put up flyers but no one had claimed the cat or ever even seen it before.

"And I live in South Philly!" she added, with the unspoken meaning: *I know all my neighbors.* "It's funny the way this cat just appeared."

She'd taken the cat in and had been caring for it—and since she worked at a vet practice she'd had her spayed and vaccinated— but she couldn't keep her because she already had a big dog and they weren't too comfortable around each other. I could adopt the cat if I wanted, she said. Would I like to come meet her?

I went to the vet's office the next day on my lunch break and met the cat, who jumped up onto a high windowsill and stared down at me. She was sprightly and slender and entirely black, with large ears like a bat and goofy, big feet. Carla, the vet tech, thought she was just under a year old, nearly grown. I liked the cat and wanted to take her home, though I wasn't entirely sure what to do with her once I did. Did cats know how to use their litter boxes on their own? I'd have to get a book.

I went back for the cat later that day, when work was out. Carla gave me one of those temporary carriers made of cardboard.

At the front desk she gave me the papers verifying the cat's vaccination status and there was a name written there.

"I've been calling her Tabitha, but you can change that," she told me. "She's your cat now."

I walked the cat the fifteen blocks to my building, fleet-footed with happiness, though she was kinda heavy. I stopped once to take a rest and I couldn't help myself: I set the carrier down on the sidewalk and opened it just enough to peek inside. The little animal looked up at me in silence.

I whispered to her, "You're my cat now."

•   •   •

I called out sick the next two days in a row, feeling like a new mother. How could I just *go to work* when I had a tiny, perfect cat friend to stare at all day long? Johanna and I kept laying the cat down on her back and watching her pop her front legs out to the sides in a hyper, eccentric way. Between that and the ears and her tiny fangs, she really did look like a bat.

I spent several hours on the phone with Maura, my dear friend from high school, consulting about names. Eventually I chose the name Trixie, even though Maura didn't think it sounded grown-up enough. To appease her, I said that Trixie's *full* name was Beatrix, after Beatrix Potter, a literary animal lover. The cat's last name, I decided, was Horovitz, because Johanna and Maura and I were married to the Beastie Boys, and since I liked the group best I got to be married to the cutest one, Ad-Rock, and that was his last name. Trixie was his love child, then, I guess. His love cat. All this made sense at the time.

For the next few months, I went to work and came home. Johanna and I watched TV and fussed over our cats. On weekends we went to the bar around the corner and fed dollars into the jukebox, then stumbled home laughing. We never did much, but our lives felt full, and I thought I was on the verge of something big all the time. But then my father died and I didn't feel like I was about to spread my wings anymore.

I went home for just a few days at first, for the funeral. A week later I took the train downtown to get more of my stuff, and eventually, on my last trip back, I collected Trixie, who had a real carrier by then. It was just a twenty-minute ride to the suburbs, but there were a lot of weird smells and the noise of the train squealing on the tracks scared her, so when we got to my parents' house—my mom's house—she hid under my old bed for hours. I'd told Johanna—and myself—that I would be back, but I couldn't think far enough into the future to guess when that might be. I ended up living back at home with my mom for the next five years.

I've always loved that house, with its deep windowsills and old-fashioned radiators that clank when the heat comes on. Trixie liked it there, too. When I took a shower in the morning, she'd run back and forth along the edge of the tub and occasionally slip and fall in. After that, I'd make my way downstairs and she'd come streaking down the staircase too, overtaking and nearly tripping me in her haste to get to *the chair*. She would then fly through the air with her front feet splayed, Spider-Man style, and land on this elegant blush-colored armchair that my dad had insisted on buying to put in the dining room, near the window, even though my mom said light-colored furniture like that would get ruined right away. Trixie did ruin it, but it took a couple years. Once attached, she'd cling to the chair and, ears back, throttle it like crazy, wild with excitement just to be alive and to be starting a new day. It made the worst ripping sound, but my mother just thought it was funny.

"Look at her, she looks like she's being buffeted by the wind!" I said one morning.

"She is being buffeted, Katie. Buffeted by her *emotions*," Mom said.

We celebrated Trixie's birthday on Halloween, because she was a black cat and because that's the day she'd appeared on Carla the vet's porch. I made her a jester's costume out of green and orange felt triangles and put it around her neck.

There was a lot of sweetness during those years, but I wasn't having the easiest time. I behaved like a bad teenager and my mom was too sad to notice. I smoked all the time and, though it's hard for me to believe it now, she let me smoke in the house. So I sat in my messy bedroom feeling lonely and stuck, dropping dead cigarette butts into mugs of cold tea. At night I went out and came home drunk. I never missed a party or a show. I didn't weigh enough back then and this gave me a kind of high too, like just huffing air was enough to keep me upright and moving through the world. I hung trendy clothing from my bones and went out, letting stupid guys burn me with their eyes. Later, I'd leave the bar alone, spilling out onto the sidewalk to catch the last train home while the people I knew or kind of knew stayed inside where it was warm and bright. If I didn't time it right I'd miss the train and have to take an expensive cab ride instead. It felt lonely, I guess, but somehow not all that alarming, to stand on a corner somewhere at one or two a.m., trying to remember— really *cogitating*, my head buzzing with beer or gin—what neighborhood I was in and where the nearest payphone was likely to be. Calling for a cab and then running to pee in a nearby alley—you can never *quite* keep it from rolling back onto your shoes—before coming back to wait for it on someone's stoop, the street as empty and haunted as a graveyard.

One way or another, I always got home intact. I'd creep through the back door into the kitchen, where Trixie was waiting for me. I'd sit at the kitchen counter, eating chips and staring at my mother's little TV, the night still ringing in my ears. Good old Trixie, she'd sit beside me on the counter—curled up in the fruit basket, if there was no fruit in it—and wait 'til it was time to go upstairs. She slept on the bed, next to my feet, and sometimes on them, every night. Even when I was too distracted or unhappy to notice her, she was there.

•   •   •

By the time I was twenty-seven, I needed to get out of my mother's house. I only got as far as an apartment in the sweet, two-story, brick building around the corner.

"You two are taking that chair with you," my mom said. We put it in the living room, with the ripped-up part facing the wall.

I was lonely in that apartment sometimes, but it was a better kind of lonely than before. I quit smoking and learned to calm the fuck down. I worked on my stories and poems and for a while there I had about two dozen pen pals. There was a giant horse chestnut tree outside my living room window, the one I had my writing desk under, and every spring it budded out into lime-green points.

I cultivated a cat-lady persona that I was proud of: I liked to think of myself as a bluestocking and a neighborhood kook, and when I wasn't hanging out with my mom I spent a lot of time alone. Still, everything I talked about was "we," as in Trixie and I. "We're gonna stay in and read tonight," I'd tell my mother, or, "Trixie and I are working on a new essay." My dearest wish was that I could take her with me everywhere I went—like to the movies and stuff—but as I liked to say back then, "The world isn't ready for our love."

Trixie had her own apartment, too. When she was young, she could still jump pretty high and she took to leaping up onto one of the shelves in my hall closet, where she would curl up on the blanket I kept there and go to sleep. I don't think I ever saw her make the jump and I still can't imagine how she did it without banging her head on the shelf above it. After a while I stopped feeling irritated that my blanket was getting covered in cat hair and replaced it with her own blankie, a miniature quilt my mom had made for her. Then I taped some "pin-ups" to the wall beside it for her to enjoy—tiny pictures of birds I'd cut out of a magazine. I've always gotten so much mileage out of my own stupid jokes.

I lived in that apartment for almost ten years. Trixie lounged in it like a queen and purred like an engine, beaming pure love energy at me with her eyes. In every room she was a loony, deadpan presence, draped over the back of the couch or on the windowsill behind the curtain, looking like one of the dark, lumpy monsters—we all know they were cats—in an Edward Gorey drawing. She was my constant companion for all those years and she even had the good grace to let me believe I lived alone.

•　　　•　　　•

How do you characterize the relationships people have with animals? They're different from the ones we have with other people, but not in every way. They're simpler; I guess that's the main thing. Cleaner. My friendship with Trixie wasn't complicated by any of the bad feelings that eventually wind their way around my human friendships: No guilt, no resentment, no jealous barbs or boring stories. We liked each other's company, as simple as that. And yet it seemed she understood and accepted me completely, too. It wasn't that she didn't notice my bad habits—that I sometimes smacked myself in the face when I felt really frustrated, or that I hung around the house too much and used my small inheritance as an excuse to not work real jobs. She just didn't care about that stuff. She had a few bad habits, too, you know. And to me, she was perfection, with her glossy fur and total serenity. She was my best friend, but she was also just a little black cat.

•　　　　•　　　　•

I've heard people say that it's not uncommon for an old pet, a cat or a dog, to die just before their person makes a major life change. Has a baby, gets married, sells the old house and moves away. My friend Sacha swears this is real, but I don't like thinking about it, since it makes me think that Trixie knew that things were about to change and thought that meant I wouldn't have room for her in my life anymore.

I'd met a guy, Joe, and fallen for him, hard. We went for drives in his car and had picnics on the grass underneath my window. He introduced me to new music, bringing me CDs he'd burned with mixes, one of which was called "Make Way for Trixie." He was always so sweet to that cat.

We'd been together for a few years when he moved to a small town in the country and I'd go visit him there on the weekend. Trixie was always fine on her own for a night. One Friday evening in February, I went with Joe to a soup cook-off that his friend was competing in. We got into a stupid argument on the drive back to his place and I wanted to go home. Going home was a big, annoying hassle though. I don't drive, so to visit him I had to take the train to the station nearest to his place, which wasn't very near at all. So I stayed and we got over whatever we were fighting about, and in the morning he drove me to the station. When I got home and let myself into my apartment, I saw Trixie lying on her side on the floor, breathing funny. Her body looked amorphous and melted, and for a confused second or two I stared, thinking it was a different cat.

At the vet's they did X-rays and couldn't see anything obstructing her lungs. But she was dying; the labored breathing was neurological and there was nothing they could do. They warned me against bringing her home, where she would only die a painful, drawn-out death. So I agreed to have her put to sleep. The process looked just the way the euphemism sounds. They gave her one shot to make her slip into a deep sleep and a second one that made her go perfectly still.

The loss hurt me so badly I disbelieved it. I must actually have been grieving my dad, who'd died the same year I got Trixie. Losing my cat must have torn open those older, deeper wounds. Right? That's what I told myself then, but I don't think that anymore. I think I just really missed my friend. Fourteen years is a long time to share a bed with somebody.

Have you ever read "Song of Myself," the Walt Whitman poem from *Leaves of Grass*? At the end, he writes about how he'll never really be gone, because after he dies he'll become the earth and the air and the water and we can look for him there, in nature. I read the ending of the poem over and over after Trixie died, and it helped. "Failing to catch me at first, keep encouraged," Walt Whitman said, and I tried to.

I also looked for comfort on the internet and found lots of people talking about how they thought they saw their animal friend around the house for weeks or months after it died. They wondered whether it was a trick of the mind or a visit from a ghost. But this never happened to me; I never thought I saw Trixie. The apartment felt like a dried-up, empty husk without her in it and I could never forget that she wasn't there.

"Missing me one place, search another."

Still, my sense of a spirit world was alarmingly strong the year after she died, as if a window between this place and the other had been left open, and I could feel the breeze. For the longest time I saw a funny image when I closed my eyes at bedtime, a picture of Trixie that was not a memory because it had never happened when she was alive. It was a picture of her standing in the sun at the head of a garden path, with tall summer growth and bright wildflowers on either side of her. She was about to step onto the path, but she didn't want to go into the garden without me; she'd paused and turned her head behind her shoulder and stayed like that, looking back at me, like an invitation.

"I stop somewhere, waiting for you."

•   •   •

I moved out of my old place a year to the day after Trixie died. I didn't do that on purpose, it was just a coincidence. I was leaving to join Joe in an apartment we'd found in that small rural town, and then we were going to get married. I'd stopped seeing that picture of Trixie in the garden, which I took to mean she finally had to go, and I had to let her.

When she died, I'd had her cremated and was given a cardboard box of her ashes. In that whole year I hadn't been brave enough to look inside it, but on the last night in my old place, late in the evening, I decided I should. I wanted to bury her ashes and some of her things out back, where she used to like to sleep in the sun while Joe and I had our picnics. I kneeled on the dry winter grass and opened the box and inside I found another box, a nice wooden one with a brass plaque with the name TRIXIE embossed on it. I'm sure I chose the thing and paid for it, but I didn't remember doing so, and seeing the box felt like a surprise, a little gift.

Out there in the dark I couldn't figure out how to open the special box, so I decided just to bury her things instead. I dug a hole with a kitchen spoon and put her collar down and covered it with dirt and I said out loud to her that I missed her but knew she'd always be with me. And I think I believe that, about everyone who lives and dies. Even if it's only in the way Walt Whitman wrote, that we'll become the dirt and the grass that grows from it, and swirl around on a stream in foam like white lace. Trixie was just a cat, but she was my friend, and I'm just a nobody, but I'm somebody too. So are you. Let's be greedy and enjoy all the surprises and little gifts, wherever we can find them. The big gifts too.

13

CROOKED CAT

ne time I found a bookstore by accident. It was a bright Saturday in May and I was taking one of my epic long walks through one of Philly's leafier neighborhoods, looking around at stuff and talking to myself, when I spotted a bookcase on the sidewalk, just sitting there. The bookcase was filled with books and it had a sign taped to it. "More this way!" it said, with an arrow underneath.

I followed its direction down a small hill, but only saw a train station housed in an old building. The front of the station faced the platform and two people were standing at the window, buying tickets for the train. The building had a green-painted trim and a low, flared roof that made it look like a house from one of those miniature Victorian Christmas villages. It was lovely. But where were the books? I kept walking and around back, I found it: A bookstore! Housed in the same building as a functioning train station! All that, plus a tortoiseshell cat in the grass out front, clearly belonging to the place. I had to go in.

Inside, the bookstore looked like something out of Tolkien—a hobbit house for books. It had low ceilings and a skinny, wonky staircase leading to the second floor. And there were books— secondhand ones—everywhere. On the bookcases, of course, but also in stacks and boxes on the floor. A big, bearded man came out of an office by the front door and beamed a quiet warmth at me. He offered me a cup of coffee—for free, like I was visiting him at his house—and we chatted while I drank it. I mentioned I'd seen a nice cat out front.

"That's C.C. Short for Crooked Cat," he said, and pointed to a page from a book of Mother Goose rhymes hanging on the wall.

There was a crooked man, and he walked a crooked mile,
He found a crooked sixpence against a crooked stile;
He bought a crooked cat, which caught a crooked mouse,
And they all lived together in a crooked little house.

I didn't ask, but I assumed the poem was chosen not because the man is crooked—he seemed to be on the straight and narrow to me—but because the building is, the old floorboards having settled in different directions over the years. I later learned that the station house is something of a treasure, designed by Frank Furness and on the National Register of Historic Places, and that the bookshop portion of the building used to be the stationmaster's quarters. Who knew stations had masters, and that the masters had quarters? Not me.

I have returned to the Crooked Mile many times since that day, almost always by myself. I've learned that C.C. lives there full-time and spends the night alone among the stacks. During business hours, she likes to sleep on the floor in a square of sunlight or on a bookshelf—at the end, like a bookend—or in a box of books, if there's room. She'll follow you around the store if she's bored and you seem interesting. And in fine weather she'll probably be outside to greet you when you arrive by rolling around in the grass and waiting for you to rub her belly.

14

OSCAR

ack when Trixie and I lived in the red brick building, the building's superintendent, Floyd, lived in the apartment beneath mine with his cat, Oscar. In the nice weather I'd see the two of them on the grounds together, Floyd rummaging around in his toolbox or in the back of his truck, and Oscar, a retiring, older cat covered in a nimbus of bright orange fur, sitting behind him.

Oscar was a great cat, and the best thing about him was that he liked to climb up the horse chestnut tree and sit in it. It was his *cattiest* trait. This enormous tree grew just outside a window in the part of my living room that I thought of as my office, because my writing desk was there. All year long I enjoyed looking at that tree from the chair where I sat working, or trying to work, or not trying at all. When it budded out every spring it was the most rousing sight to see—thousands of tiny sprouts in a pastel lime green, the promise of good things to come. But the thing that made me happiest was when I'd be typing away at my computer and notice some *other* color out of the corner of my eye, and I'd have to turn my head to see for sure: Yes! There was Oscar again, nestled up high in the tree, his carroty shade giving him away every time. I swear, if he'd been any other color it wouldn't have been half as funny.

I think these visitations wouldn't have meant as much to me if I hadn't lived alone, but the world seems more capricious when you spend a lot of time by yourself. The scary things are scarier, but the nice things feel so much sweeter. Every surprise seemed like a message from the universe: *You're not really alone.* Like the perfect, rounded bird's nest in the shrub out front, hidden by leaves all summer and then revealed one day in autumn when the branches were suddenly bare, like an unwrapped gift. Or the time I found a few quarters glued to the sidewalk, a prank that was more thought-provoking than mean, and made me wonder if the trickster was hiding nearby to watch me try to pull the coins off the pavement and chuckle about what a greedy fucker I was.

Or a bright orange cat sitting high in a tree, calm as you like, looking like a giant berry that had sprouted off the end of one branch.

15

SNICKERDOODLE

nicks is a rag-tag, former stray with a limp from a busted hip and a sneaky alley cat attitude, but she was once a cover model.

My sister Liz adopted Snicks from Animal Control in Philadelphia, where she's a volunteer. The poor cat, a raggedy ginger, had come in with a badly broken leg and promptly got a nasty cold. The organization is so overburdened that when an animal is very hurt or sick they have to consider euthanasia as a real possibility.

Liz panicked. She already had two cats in her small house and didn't need another, but she couldn't stand the thought of anything happening to this one. A doctor who volunteers with the shelter did the surgery needed to fix the cat's leg, then sent her home with Liz to recuperate. When I first saw her, she was in triage in the small second bedroom that Liz used as an office, lying awkwardly in a cardboard box with a towel in it. The fur on one back leg was shaved up to her tail and it was white like a chicken leg at the supermarket. The room smelled bad in an unidentifiable, sick way, like a hospital room. But Snickerdoodle is such an excitable thing, when I walked in she sprang to her feet and hurried over to me, hobbling dramatically on the bad leg. She wasn't supposed to put pressure on it, so we talked gently to her until she was calm, then picked her up and put her back in the box.

After a few months the leg was healed and covered in a downy orange. In a year, Snickerdoodle was the picture of health, with a full coat and a fat bushy tail like a fox. Liz decided to enter her in the fundraiser photo contest that Animal Control runs every year. People who have adopted animals from the shelter can submit photos of them and everyone who makes a donation can vote for their favorite. The top twelve animals are featured in a calendar and the pet with the most votes gets the cover. Each time you donate, you get another vote.

Liz was determined that her cat would win. Everyone got into the spirit. Joe and I made a few donations each and so did my mom. On the last night of the contest, it was down to Snickerdoodle and a funny little white poodle named Hamilton. In his photo, Hamilton was looking up into the camera, fairly begging for you to love him. Liz wanted Snickerdoodle to blow Hamilton out of the water. She sat at home all evening, sending in money via Paypal and refreshing the website over and over again to see if Snicks was in the lead.

"Fuckin' Hamilton!" she texted me. "People keep voting for his scruffy ass!"

I don't know how much money she sank into this project, but it was enough to win. Snickerdoodle would have her portrait taken by a professional photographer, then be featured on the calendar's cover, as well as in any promotional materials the shelter put out that year. Joe and I were excited: A cat we knew was going to become famous and we had ourselves to thank! But Liz told me that after all that, she felt guilty for being so aggressive toward the poor, sweet dog.

"Gee," she said, after the excitement had died down. "I feel sort of bad now."

16

OWLBERT

You might already know about Owlbert. On the internet, his tagline is "Part cat, part owl, all mustache," because he's huge and fluffy and mostly grey with a prominent, white, handlebar-shaped fur mustache. He looks like one of those enormous skeins of expensive yarn that was hand-spun, with some parts all tufty like cotton candy and others almost crimped with curls. *Boucle*, I think it's called. He's a *boucle* cat. He's kind of a big deal. Someone made a mockumentary about him and gave it a whispery voiceover that spoofs Werner Herzog. Do yourself a favor and watch it on his fan page at Facebook.com/OwlbertTheCat. It's a hoot. (Pun intended.)

The reason *I* know about Owlbert is because I know his human companion, Pi, a hilarious punk rock librarian who used to live in Philadelphia. Though we've never been close, I've known her for a long time now. The day I met her we were in the kitchen at some house party in South Philly to which she had worn a t-shirt with a diagram of the female endocrine system on it and the slogan THE INTERNET: A SERIES OF TUBES. She and I would bump into each other at zine fairs and bars now and then, and even someone's wedding once, and we always had good talks.

I got to meet Owlbert once. Pi had broken her leg and it was winter, so she'd been housebound and wanted some company. But mostly it was understood that I was there to visit her new cat. When I arrived, Pi was propped up with pillows on her bed and Owlbert was right there with her, curled up tight and perched primly on her midsection like the cherry on a sundae. Like I said, Pi and I weren't close, and it might have been weird of me to march right into her bedroom after walking through the front door, but that's what I did. I sat down on the bed next to her and started cooing to that big ball of fluff.

Her apartment was one of the best looking ones I've ever been in. She had a formica kitchen set that looked like it belonged in a diner in a movie from the 50s, *Star Trek* figures posed along her bookshelves, and tons of Rocket from the Crypt show posters, all bold colors and cartoon pin-up chicks. The whole place was crammed with interesting stuff and it was in high contrast to the winter colors of her block in South Philly. I remember leaving there to catch my bus—*grey sidewalk grey buildings grey sky*—my head filled with sensations, the memory of Owlbert's magnificent mane among them. A year or two later Pi and Owlbert moved out to sunny California, so these days the only way I can visit him—I mean them—is on the internet, like the rest of his fans.

ubh was a pretty, long-haired cat I lived with in Ireland, where I spent a year in my 20s attempting (and failing) to get a graduate degree in literature. The cat's name was pronounced "dove," sort of, but more like "doov," like the vowel in the word "foot." It's the Irish word for black, and she was named for her color. "Dubh" is the same word found in the name Dublin, which is Irish for "black pool," in case you wanted to know.

Dubh was a pet, I guess, but she had much more freedom than the average house cat. She spent nearly all her time stalking the neighborhood. Her owner, Ian—he was more like her concierge than her owner, truthfully, though he was the owner of the house and my landlord—rarely knew where she was. He didn't let the cat sleep with him, but she often snuck in under the quilt on my bed when she was supposed to be outside. I started feeling itchy all the time; I'm pretty sure she had fleas.

Ian's house was a "worker's cottage" in an old working class neighborhood north of Dublin's center. The cottages were built to house the employees of the nearby Guinness plant and they lined one street in a compact row. I rented a tiny bedroom from him and he and I shared the rest of the tiny cottage, which consisted of a tiny front room, a tiny kitchen, and a tiny bathroom. Originally the house had just three rooms, but at one point a modern kitchen was added, along with a sliding glass door onto an excessively tiny back deck. Ian was an English guy in his late 40s, pompous as could be, but nice enough when all was said and done.

One morning Ian and I stood in his kitchen, drinking coffee. As we talked, he glanced behind my head and started to smile, and I turned around to see the cat through the glass, creeping low and silent along the deck railing like a jungle predator. It was the first time we'd seen her in days. Ian dropped his voice to an Attenborough whisper and narrated, "The noble, savage beast makes her way to the nearest garbage pail." He could be funny sometimes.

18

HONEYBUNCH

hat can you say about a cat named Honeybunch? She was delightful. A fluffy princess of a cat who lived in the house next door to my mother's, she was black all over with a white chest, and had those curly whiskers long-haired cats sometimes have.

The woman who owned Honeybunch is a huge cat lover—she can be standoffish and hard to read, but she always brightened up at the mention of her cat. Her husband, Jon, had less patience for Honeybunch's antics. Their kitchen window is just across from my mother's and the houses are so close together that it's kind of *right there*. On many occasions as we sat around the table talking, my mother and I witnessed the cat trying to get back inside her house. First she'd cry at the back door, and when that didn't work she'd go stand on the front porch and cry there for a while. And when *that* didn't work, she'd walk around to the side of the house, leap up to the kitchen window, and cling to the screen with her claws. To our great amusement, Jon, if he was alone in the kitchen, would whack the screen with his hand and send the cat flying. It was the only response that stunt ever got, so I can't imagine why the cat kept trying it. Mom and I had to bite our lips every time it happened because Jon would totally have heard us laughing from next door.

Poor Honeybunch. She made the best of her time outside, though. One year, my mother had a patio installed over part of her yard so that she could sit out back and drink her morning coffee when the weather was mild. She kept this pleasant routine for a while before Honeybunch decided to participate. The cat liked to creep into my mother's yard, jump onto her lap, and fall asleep. If my mom was in one of her reclining chairs, Honeybunch would climb up higher and curl up on her chest instead, feather duster tail right in my mother's face.

When Honeybunch died, my mom's neighbor was crushed, and my mother had tears in her eyes, too, when she told me about it. I guess life on the patio was a little lonelier after that.

19

CHACHI

Do you remember Chachi from *Happy Days*? Fonzi's sexy younger cousin who wore t-shirts with no sleeves and a red bandana tied around his denim thigh? Who thought he was hot shit because he *was* hot shit? I had the biggest crush on him. Too bad Scott Baio grew up to be such a gross loser.

I wasn't the only one who loved Chachi. I mean, Joanie loved Chachi, famously. So did my friend Alyssa. She and I worked together at an "alternative" newspaper and went out together at least weekly. We didn't get paid too well at that job, but we had the hook-up to all the best shows and bars because those venues were our advertisers. Our Christmas party was always a downtown hipster affair at a club or some trendy new restaurant. I wouldn't consider that suitable compensation for my work nowadays, but I was pretty silly when I was twenty-five. Alyssa and I would get ready to go out together—radio blaring while she did my makeup—and I always crashed at her house afterward. Alyssa has a lot of qualities I admire, one of which is her flagrant love of things that are cheesy. Prom queen tiaras, sweet mixed drinks, big Jersey girl hair. She was the prom queen, but she could also do an impression of Glenn Danzig barking into the mic with one foot up on the amp that was totally on-point. That's just who she is. So she named her dear cat Chachi in honor of her love for the boy Chachi, which I consider an excellent choice.

Chachi the cat was a big blonde tabby with a super chill personality, the kind of cool cat you hoped would choose you to pay attention to over a room full of other people, thereby bestowing his cool on you. Sometimes he came and sat with me and sometimes he snubbed me for somebody else. No hard feelings, Chachi, I get it—when you've got looks *and* personality there's not always enough of you to go around.

The best thing that Chachi did was sleep in a bed like a person. Many was the skull-cracking hangover morning that I woke up early to catch the train home, but first went in to whisper a goodbye to the two of them, Alyssa and Chach, asleep side-by-side in her bed with their heads on separate pillows like an old married couple.

20

THE LANDLORD'S CATS

I told you about my superintendent, Floyd, right? The one whose cat Oscar liked to sit in the tree? Floyd was an older guy, maybe about 70, and he'd lived pretty hard for most of his life. He could be a pain in the ass, a typical neighborhood guy with a lot of loudmouth opinions, but I was fond of him. Sometimes I'd see flashes of irritability that I'm sure were just shadows of what he'd get like during his drinking days. But he was always kind to me, affectionate even. One of the nicest things about him was how much he loved his cats. For a while there were three. First he had Oscar, and later he got this swaggerish tuxedo cat named Pepe. Then a third one came along, a pretty, silver cat whose fur looked almost blue. He had a small, stocky build and a sweet round head. Floyd named the cat Sable, "because of his color," but then somebody told him that "sable" meant brown and he changed the name to Smoky.

Floyd had found Smoky hanging around a dumpster looking for food, and the cat looked so pitiful and scrawny that he took him home. Soon the cat was sleek and healthy, and he was a friendly soul, always butting his head against your leg to get your attention. He never lost that touch of wildness, though. His eyes gleamed differently than the house cats I was used to, burning with just a little more life.

Floyd got sick with a cancer of the stomach and he talked about it freely, pointing to his terrible distended belly with an amused sort of disbelief. "I don't know how you women can stand it!" he'd say, as if carrying a baby was the same thing as having a big ball of poison inside you. His personality was as bombastic as ever, but he looked older, faded, without his hair. After half a year or so of this, I bumped into the plumber in the hallway and he said he'd seen Floyd moving out that morning. Moving out? That couldn't be right. I figured something bad had happened, and sure enough, Floyd had been moved into hospice care. For several weeks I got reports on his health from the owner of our building, who lived in a nice house up the street, and then Floyd died.

I wanted to take care of his cats. I'd been thinking about it while Floyd was dying at the hospice. Those cats already had the run of the property; I wouldn't have to change much about their lives or take on a lot of responsibility, I figured. And somehow it seemed important to keep some aspect of Floyd alive around the place. I thought about the pine tree that grew in the center of the courtyard and how Floyd had told me that he got permission to plant it there when his daughter died, to remember her. He strung colored lights around it every year at Christmas.

I didn't know how to make good on my cat care offer, exactly—the cats weren't mine to take, and I couldn't make my promise to Floyd since no one could talk to him anymore. So I kept telling Patty that if there was "anything I could do, like look after the cats," I would.

Oh yeah, Floyd had a girlfriend. Her name was Patty and she lived in the building too, but in her own place. I liked her well enough. She once sent a fan letter about my writing to the newspaper I wrote for, without admitting that she knew me personally, a memory that makes me both smile and squirm with embarrassment. She accepted my offers to help her clear out Floyd's (truly alarming amount of) hoarded junk in the basement while he was still in hospice care, since she was the only one around who could put his meager affairs in order and she wasn't young herself. But whenever I mentioned the cats, she just smiled politely and didn't say anything about them one way or the other.

And then the day after he died, the *very next fucking day*, the cats disappeared. Patty gave them away. My downstairs neighbor, Adelaide, told me, looking stunned. Patty didn't tell anybody in the building what she was planning to do. She just gathered them up in her little car and drove them to the pound. Poor Adelaide was bereft. I felt terrible about it too, and it was a worse kind of terrible than the simple sadness I felt about Floyd dying. It was that dirty kind of longing you feel when you don't get to make peace with something, a nagging pain that never heals. In this case it was a small pain, I guess, a hangnail of the heart.

I avoided Patty after that. I was polite when I saw her, and when she asked, I helped her dispose of the 16 million half-full paint cans Floyd had left in yet another corner of the basement. But I didn't feel safe around her anymore. A couple times she knocked on my door and I held still and didn't answer. And when she moved away from the building a few months later, she didn't tell anyone about that either. One day, she was just gone.

•   •   •

But that's not the end of the story of Floyd's cats.

One late summer evening I was walking through the neighborhood on my way home. To get there from the train station, I walked past a low, stone wall that ran the length of a block. Behind the wall, set up on a hill and hidden by trees, there was a house, and the growth of pachysandra and other vines on the wall itself was thick. It was like the suburban version of walking on a path alone through an enchanted wood. I walked quietly, my mind full of nonsense as always, when I heard a rustling sound just beside my head. I was only about six inches taller than the wall, so the sound seemed to whisper in my ear. I didn't think much about it—some squirrel or bird, who knows—but a moment later a funny sprite of a grey cat popped its head out of the pachysandra and looked at me. It was playing with me. It was—holy shit, it was Smoky! Floyd and the cats had been gone for months and I'd mostly stopped thinking about them. But here he was, as silent and mischievous as ever, and he seemed to shimmer, the same color as the silver-blue moonlight, like he was a dancing reflection of the moon on a lonely black lake. I laughed and grabbed the cat's head in a tousle and he nudged me. Then he ran ahead, stopped, jumped down from the wall onto the sidewalk in front of me, and led me all the way home.

I saw the cat a handful of times after that, and each time he seemed to be surprising me on purpose. I spotted him back behind my building, strolling around and ducking behind parked cars, like Smoky used to do. I saw him at night again too, twice more, and in that same fairytale way the cat led me around, looking back and teasing, egging me on to follow him, his eyes vivid in the dark. He looked like Smoky, he acted like Smoky—Smoky had come back, and there was no one I could tell. It was my secret. (I did tell my mom, actually, breathless, the morning after the first time I saw the cat. I don't think she believed me, though.) He appeared just a few more times before he disappeared again, and I didn't know what that meant either. Maybe one of my neighbors took him inside and started calling him their pet. Maybe he had come back looking for Floyd, the way I've read that cats and dogs do—you know those stories, the beloved pet runs away after a long-distance move and finds its way back to the old house, despite the incredible odds against it—maybe he'd come back and hung around a while to see if Floyd was still there, and not finding him, decided to go back to his new home, wherever that was.

I know it was probably a different cat. I know that. Lots of people had pet cats in the neighborhood, and there were always a few strays around too. And let's face it, one cat can look an awful lot like another. But my heart still thuds when I remember that night and the nights that followed when Smoky appeared to me and brisked along beside me in the dark, teasing me, silent, like something in a dream. I can remember how much I wanted it to be true, that this bright little being wasn't dead, put to sleep in some shelter, that he wasn't gone from my life at all, that he remembered me the way I remembered him and had come back to his old home just to say hello.

21

THE GHOST KITTEN

uring the warm months, Joe and I like to keep our front door open for a breeze. Our house is narrow and has three downstairs rooms, one behind the other. If we leave open the front door and one of the windows in the back, we get a gorgeous cross-breeze. One time last summer, late in the evening, I got up to shut the door after it had finally gotten dark. I stood in the doorway and looked out onto the street first. It was nice for July. It was hot alright, but the air was moving, and yellow lights still glowed behind some of the windows up and down the block. Almost before I had a chance to see it, a tiny animal, light-colored, darted down the sidewalk to my right and disappeared under a parked car. I yelled into the house.

"Joe! I saw a kitten!"

This is just the kind of announcement Joe likes to hear. He hurried to the door as quietly as he could, jumped into a pair of flip-flops he keeps there, and went out to see what he could. He squatted down beside the car I pointed to and at that, the white flash took off again. Joe hauled ass up the street after it, and once I'd pulled the door shut behind me I joined him. Up the steep, steep hill our house is on—we've lived here for a year now and I *still* feel my thighs burning every time I hike up it—we chased this tiny ball of cotton-puff from parked car to parked car. When a streetlight caught the kitten, I could see it had a halo of wispy, white fuzz around its body; it must have been very young. Every time I spotted it I let out a yelp. It was *that cute*, and so hard to catch.

It went on like that for ages. Once my eyes adjusted to the dark I saw more and more cats out there, sitting on steps, hiding behind plant pots, strolling across the street. I must have taken on a cat's mind that night as I searched for the kitten. I felt like one of them, moving through the dark like liquid, the air as warm as bathwater. The unspoken thing between Joe and I as we worked together, chasing each other and a stray kitten up and up the street, was that we wanted a cat. I'd been without a cat since Trixie died, and his dear old cat Georgia had died only a few months earlier and he wasn't ready for another one yet; he'd said so several times. I hadn't been pushing him, though I had mentioned that I thought our house would be awfully cozy with a cat in it by the time winter came. We hadn't discussed it any more than that.

And yet here we were, trying to get ourselves a new cat on a thick, gooey Philadelphia summer night. The side of my face rested on the pebbly pavement at one point; I'd pressed my body down flat on the dirty sidewalk and stretched my arm all the way out, trying to reach the kitten where it sat under a car. If only I could stretch far enough to pluck it up in my hand, Joe would let me keep it; I knew he would. He would want the cat, too. But we were so outmatched, we'd never catch it. This little animal had lived its whole brief life this way, flying silent, staying safe by slipping into tiny holes in the fabric of existence.

We didn't stop chasing the cat because we ran out of energy—to be honest, I didn't want our adventure to end even after I'd gotten totally winded—but we lost sight of it finally and had to give up. After that night, we never saw it again.

22

BACKYARD SAGA: THE BAD MAMMER JAMMER

The Bad Mammer Jammer looks like a freaking *panther*. I can see him right now. I'm sitting on my chair in the kitchen, looking at him, and he is sitting on one of the wooden planks that frames our garden, looking around the yard, when he *slowwwly* swings his head to face the window, looking at me. His eyes glow yellow, and he only blinks once he's broken my gaze and turned away.

The Bad Mammer Jammer is huge and black and sleek, with a big head and big feet. He looks more wild than the other strays we see around here, some of whom act like they used to be people's pets. Not this guy. When he moves, he prowls, keeping his head and tail low. Not only that, but I think he's the father of the kitten we've been attempting to look after. He's the only cat that the Mama ever allows near her and her baby—the one remaining kitten—who have taken to sometimes sleeping in the cardboard shelter I made for them. When she's lying in the grass watching the kitten romp around, he might decide to join her from the yard next door—taking his sweet time, of course, with his Wild Kingdom swagger.

Two nights ago the temperatures dropped into the single digits. Our bedroom walls were cold to the touch, and when we got up in the morning we saw thick ice covering the window. This morning I went downstairs to start the coffee and the kitchen floor was as cold as a skating rink on my bare feet. When I opened the back door to toss some cans into the recycling bin, the noise scared the Mama, the Bad Mammer Jammer, *and* the kitten, who came tearing out of the shelter one after the other. I was amazed they could all fit in there. I can't always tell if the cats back there are safe and comfortable, but they do seem to have formed a family of sorts.

23

EMMA & DEE

ee and Emma brought Joe and I together, sort of. He and I had met a year earlier at a zine fair in New Jersey, where he lived. We'd remained friends for months, emailing and talking on the phone, and even made a zine together. I wrote something silly about how my dream is to one day put my arms around a big bird and hug it, and Joe drew pictures of me embracing a turkey and an ostrich.

Then summer came and Joe told me he'd be spending a week in Philadelphia to look after his sister's cats. He asked if I wanted to go out to dinner with him when he was in town and my stomach did an unpleasant flip. That's how I realized I liked him, even more than I thought I did.

I took the bus downtown and met him at a pub, where we ate and talked and got rip-snorting drunk on wine (or at least I did). Afterward, we roamed the neighborhood, looking at the nice houses and sometimes holding hands. That part of the city, just south of downtown, is so pretty. There are several blocks called garden blocks, with the houses on either side of the street facing each other and a pedestrian walkway with huge gardens down the center. In the summer, the garden blocks were shockingly fragrant in the dark.

Back at Joe's sister's place, we put on some music and negotiated our lingering shyness by fussing over her cats. Dee is the baby—an unusual, adorable, anime-looking cat with enormous eyes—

and Emma is her mother. Joe's sister adopted them at the same time. Her boyfriend was the one who named Emma, which turned out to be short for M.L.B., as in Major League Baseball. Dee liked to race through the small apartment like a bat out of hell. Her favorite toy was a plastic fork. If you tossed one on the floor, she'd tear down the hallway toward it, leap on it, and go sliding under a throw rug with it. This led to the second phase of the game, in which Dee hid the fork from herself, then stalked it. She'd throw herself on her side and rummage around under the rug for the fork, then go insane with excitement when she could hear it moving against the floor.

I got tipsy and let the night wear on, but if I stayed too long I'd miss my train and have to stay over, a thought which terrified me. I said goodbye just in time to catch the last train home and ran all the way to the station, my boots clopping on the sidewalk like horses' hooves. Now Joe and I are married and we play with Dee and Emma whenever we visit his sister, who also married that dude she was dating. So I guess you could say Dee and Emma brought them together, too. Cats are really something, aren't they?

24

CORNBREAD

Joe and I love to go on road trips, so after we got married that's what we did. We rented a car and drove down south, from New Jersey all the way to the Gulf Coast.

In planning our trip we looked for cities and towns we'd never been to, and instead of staying in hotels we rented apartments and houses we found listed online. We tried to choose ones that seemed special in some way. In Asheville we picked a place called the Sassy Pink Cottage, and in Athens we found a one-story house with a screened-in porch and a pawpaw tree out front. Reviewers of the Athens house mentioned the wood floors and lazy ceiling fans—and, frequently and fondly, Cornbread the cat. We were sold. Off we went.

In Annapolis, Maryland we picked our way over cobblestone streets in the rain, listening to a woman in a cape tell us ghost stories about the colonial town. In North Carolina we drove through the Blue Ridge Mountains, and they were misty and majestic and pristine. I thought of the Civil War and the Foxfire books, homesteaders and potbelly stoves, but the only people we actually met were the friendly women at the thrift store where we bought a Gameboy and some DVDs.

In Birmingham we stayed with my pen pal, Burgin, who I'd never met in person, except for once, when I Skyped with his high school English class to talk about writing. Burgin was a lovely host. He took us out and got us drunk and put us up in his cottage, which was festooned with show posters and crammed with records, CDs, and books. On our second night there, all three of us, me, Joe, and Burgin, gave a reading in a refabbed industrial space downtown. I liked that city. It was hardscrabble and tough, but feisty and thriving in the face of its decay. It reminded me of Philadelphia, only much hotter.

And throughout all these adventures, for close to two weeks, we looked forward to getting to Athens and meeting the cat we hoped to befriend there. Because of his name, Cornbread came to represent everything we'd imagined and hoped the South would be. We talked about him every day in the car. "Do you think Cornbread will sleep on the bed with us?" I'd say, and, "I wonder what Cornbread looks like." I couldn't help picturing a cat with a squarish build and buttery yellow fur.

Cornbread turned out to be a light orange color, not too different from what I'd imagined. He lived with his owner, Billy, and Billy's young family in the larger house next door. The cat didn't sleep with us, but I did get to see him one morning, after I heard Joe's voice coming through the open window. He'd gone out for coffee and on his way back he bumped into Billy (and his famous cat) on the small lawn next door. I pushed aside the curtain and saw the three of them there, Cornbread creeping around behind the two men, hunting something in a shrub, his tail twitching. The ceiling fan turned sleepily over my head.

"Hey 'Bread," I could hear Billy say. "Come meet the honeymooners!"

25

PUNKHOUSE CAT FIGHT

This was so embarrassing. One summer night, Joe and I drove to a house that was tucked away in the suburban woods of South Jersey to see the singer-songwriter David Bazan play. He was on one of his so-called living room tours, where people apply to book him to play at their house; like their actual house where they live. It was an awesome show. Really intimate and raw, which is the best way to hear his music, I think. Just him banging on his beautiful gleaming guitar, singing his guts out.

After the show, everyone quietly ambled out back and some folks got in their cars to go, but Joe and I lurked around like creeps because we wanted to talk to him and give him some zines (well, Joe did). I felt awkward about it because I hate meeting people whose work I admire. How do I tell them I like what they do without sounding like a groveling fan? It's impossible. We couldn't find a way in anyway because he was thronged by horrible fanboys who just wanted to hear themselves brag that they knew what kind of gear he'd used at every show since 1999.

Joe and I tried to play it cool by squatting down and fussing over these friendly but slightly aggressive cats that had started weaving around our legs and butting their heads into us. Eventually David noticed us there and said something chummy to us about the cats, which was our "in"—we looked up at him and smiled and acted like we just casually hang out with our music heroes every day. Joe went to stand up and talk to him properly, and it was at that very moment that the two cats I'd been patting started to fight. One of them got its claws stuck in the back of my shirt and let out an almighty screech, and they both started twisting around back there, attacking each other and catching my skin with their claws as they went. It was dark in the yard, so I chuckled effacingly instead of yelping in pain and just hoped that no one could see that this noisy event was taking place, like, *on* my body.

The worst thing about all of this was that the fanboys had created an atmosphere of awkwardness that was impenetrable. The catfight was the sort of thing I might have laughed at under normal circumstances, and David Bazan seems like a nice, easy-going guy, but we all felt stiff and uncomfortable because the fans were trying so hard to seem cool that no one knew what to do or say. They just stood there, deciding with their hive mind not to acknowledge my predicament. So I let Joe do his thing and extracted myself from the fight as gracefully as I could, a move that unfortunately included me losing my footing and slipping forward into the dirt for a second. But we ended up walking away from there feeling pretty pleased with ourselves. I was proud of Joe. He was brave enough to introduce himself to one of his idols, not in some weird, worshipful way, but as one artist to another, and that is no small thing.

26

GRAYSON

A few summers ago, Joe bought tickets to see a musician we both like play a small show in Indiana. 800 miles from home, just for the heck of it. We sat around his hotbox of an apartment one afternoon, plotting out our driving route, when I had an idea. If we booked a few readings to do along our way, our trip would be more than just a vacation.

"Why don't we go on tour!?" I said. I'd always wanted to go on tour. It frustrates me that my life as a writer isn't more fabulous, and I'm jealous of musicians, who get to live on the road and plug into that crazy energy the audience generates every night. I want costumes and crowds, and way more photographic evidence of my existence. A zine tour might not make us rock stars, but it was a step in the right direction.

Our first stop was Pittsburgh because I knew someone there, a writer named Karen who I met years ago on Myspace. (Myspace!) Karen is cool, a very good writer and a big community organizer who is always dreaming up new projects—like Small Press Roulette, in which you sign up to receive a surprise package of zines, journals, and magazines she compiles for you. Karen kindly organized a reading for us and offered to put us up at her house, provided we didn't mind her cats, which she knew I wouldn't since she'd once spent an uncomfortable night at my place when *she* was on tour. I slept on the couch that night so that she could have my bed, but I'm pretty sure that Trixie hogged it.

The reading she set up for us was in a pretty coffee shop that was buzzing with people and movement. The day we arrived in Pittsburgh, we met her there and the three of us stood in the back of the room and took turns reading to a small crowd. It was warm that evening, and from where I stood I could see down the block through the cafe's open doors. My memory of that night is of big trees making a canopy over the sidewalk and the streetlights all glowing and blurry in the soft summer air. After the reading, we went out and drank cheap beers and ate pierogies in a dive bar, and I let myself feel proud of having pulled this off.

That night, Joe and I tucked ourselves in on the floor of Karen's front room, which was practically soundproofed by the sheer number of books in it. Lying down, our bodies took up most of the floor, and tall bookcases guarded us all around. We were very snug. And after driving across the state of Pennsylvania and getting nervous over doing the reading, we were exhausted. I slept so hard I didn't notice if any of Karen's cats pestered us during the night. To be honest, I don't remember much about those cats at all, just that the grey one was called Grayson, which I thought was cute. Apparently the book room was where he preferred to sleep, but he politely left it for us guests that night.

Karen and her boyfriend crept out of the house to go to work early the next morning, letting us sleep in. When I woke up, the house felt loud with silence, and I sat up and watched dust motes float around for a while before I realized they'd probably already left. After brewing coffee in their small kitchen and filling up our travel mugs, we left too, and pulled the door shut on their sweet house, made cozy by cats and books.

27

NEIL YOUNG

I knew Neil for some time before I learned that his *full name* is Neil Young. Finding this out made me like him even more than I already did.

Neil is a large, long-haired, orange tabby with a wide, mournful face. He's magnificent looking. A friend once said that he looks like an angry Japanese god, and it's true: He looks like one of those masks with the downturned mouth, expressive eyebrows, and flowing mustache. I've heard he can be grumpy too, but have never seen any evidence of this myself.

Neil belongs to my friends Eva and Lily, who have been a couple since college. Neil has been with Lily even longer. When she adopted him from the pound in high school, he already had the name Cornelius, but she thought it didn't quite suit him. So they took to calling him Neil for short, and at one point it occurred to teenage Lily that she could make the name a tribute to a musician she loved. And so he became Neil Young, the cat. Lily finds it amusing to hear the vet tech call out to the waiting room, "Are the owners of Neil Young here?"

These days Lily and Eva and Neil live in a jewel box of an Art Deco apartment building on a tree-lined street in West Philadelphia. It's the kind of place Wes Anderson might dream up—a sort of fantasy of bygone city living, with a tidy, elegant courtyard in front, a small babbling fountain, and a black, wrought-iron gate. The elevator has a gate, too, the kind you have to pull across the doorway before the outer door will shut. Neil Young doesn't go outside; he lounges on a white radiator cover under the window, where he can feel the warmth of the heating in the winter and the sun in the summer and listen to the murmuring of the fountain all year round.

28

GWEN

For a while after college, Joe lived back at home with his parents, and for about a year his older brother Tommy, and Tommy's girlfriend Michelle, lived there too. Tommy, Michelle, and Gwen.

Gwen is huge, with long, soft, grey fur. Even when she's sitting down she looks tall, and in the past she has weighed as much as twenty-two pounds, though she was never really overweight. They all lived together back when the cat was young, but she was already formidable, and one of her pastimes was stalking Joe around his parents' house. He'd see her hunting him and hurry into another room, and when he turned back he'd see Gwen's face, peering at him from behind the door. He'd laugh and run into a different room, and when he turned to look there she'd be, hiding and looking around a corner. When she eventually caught up with him, she'd run at him and take a flying leap toward his torso, so he could either catch her in his arms or get clobbered. It was funny because she was still small, and no one knew she'd grow to be so big and remain every bit as rambunctious.

Once, Tommy and Michelle went away for a week and the cat was upset by it. Joe made a special effort to be sweet to her, easing up on their usual rough-housing and feeding her tons of treats. Gwen really took to him after that. Toward the end of that week, she joined him where he was stretched out on the couch, snuggled down beside him, and held his head in her paws, claws ever so slightly extended. She then groomed his hair with her tongue, and every time he tried to squirm away she held his head more firmly, her claws poking his scalp like a warning. This grooming session only lasted for about ten minutes, but it was pretty gross. Joe Googled it and read that he had somehow entered into a "sibling" relationship with the cat, which was why she chased, attacked, and groomed him that time, when she needed some comforting.

29

RICKY

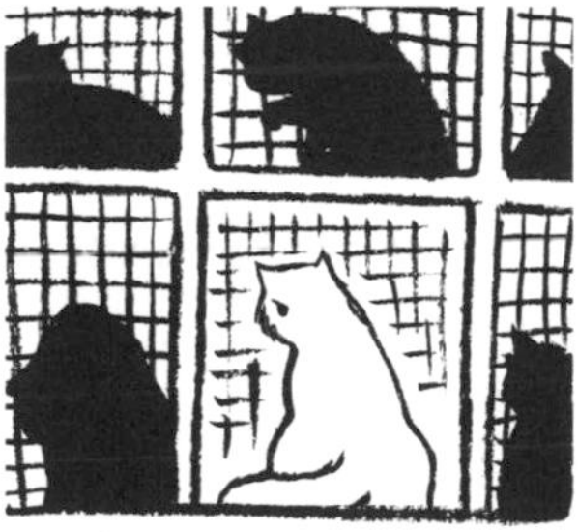

L ike I said, when I first met Joe he was living at home with his parents, where he'd been since he graduated from college. I'm ten years older than he is, which meant that in some ways I was in a different phase of life than he was. But in truth, I hadn't strayed far from home either—I lived in an apartment just a few blocks from the house I grew up in, and where my mother still lived, and we saw or talked to each other almost every single day. Dating a guy who lived at home with his parents didn't feel as weird to me as it might have to another thirty-something lady.

Still, he wanted to move out as soon as he was able to, and I agreed. It was time. He got a job as a tutor and paid off his loans, and once he could afford to move he found an apartment in a small town in New Jersey, about an hour's drive into the country and away from the congested eastern-seaboard nightmare where he grew up. People think all of New Jersey is a nightmare like that, all strip malls and pollution and wall-to-wall traffic, but it's not. It's so beautiful out in the country. Joe's adopted town was right on the rugged Delaware, and surrounding it were farms, patches of woods, and other tiny settlements along the river, most of them former mill towns.

Joe's place was in a rickety old wooden building on Main Street. It was too cold in the winter and too hot in the summer and all his neighbors were oddballs, but it was cozy there. There was a bike shop downstairs, and during business hours (and sometimes after) we could hear the owner's classic rock vibrating in the floorboards. Main Street turned into a small bridge that went over the river, and it was even more rural across the way on the Pennsylvania side. In summer, on Saturdays, Joe and I would walk over the bridge to buy produce and cut flowers from the family farm there.

When he first moved in, though, it was January, and that's a lonely time of year to go off somewhere on your own. It was his first experience living alone and he liked the independence, the eating-spaghetti-in-your-undies-ness of having his own place, but something was missing. He needed a buddy. He didn't think of himself as a cat person, but he'd come to love my cat Trixie, and he knew how much it had meant to me to have her friendship in an apartment that would have been awfully quiet without her. Maybe he'd check out the local shelter, just to see.

He told me about his visit to the SPCA, a rural one that was different from the pounds where his family had always gotten their dogs. This place had a couple of ancient-looking horses in a ring out front, and the dogs and cats were inside, separated into two different halves of the building. A volunteer took him to the two cat rooms: Males in one and females in the other. He didn't have a preference so he visited both, patting as many cats as he could and laughing at their antics. He said there was one cat, named Ricky, who he thought he liked the best, but he wanted me to meet him before he decided.

I took the train out to the station closest to town and he came to pick me up in his old Maxima, which had so little shock absorbency that it felt like riding in a Conestoga wagon. We enjoyed the drive to the shelter anyway, the same way we enjoyed every drive out there, flying past farms and tiny country churches, old graveyards with crooked stones, small stands of woods and huge stark winter skies. I've never learned to drive a car, and even though I know it sounds like a bad way to live your life—metaphorically, I mean—I really love being a passenger. There's something so sweet about having permission to do nothing but sit and look and think. I played with the radio and let my mind drift from thought to thought, my heart lifting with each new view.

The shelter was at the end of a long dirt drive, and even from the car I could see it was a miserable place. We stopped to look for the horses before we went in and I spotted one, which was actually a stocky miniature horse that looked more like a mule and had mean, yellow teeth. The poor creature looked pitiful there, alone in his ring, which had a sign stapled to one of its posts:

WATCH WHERE YOU PUT YOUR FINGERS. I'M A LI'L NIPPER!

Inside, I was impressed by how different the energy in the two cat rooms was. The female room was cozy and inviting, with cats curled up neatly, perched like hens all around the floor and windowsills and inside their cages. The male room was taut with vitality. There were house cats as well as barn cats, and the barn cats were feral—wild and unsweet—stalking around on the tops of the cages near the ceiling. In the middle of all that commotion, Joe went over to Ricky. He was a big, gorgeous old fella with the regal carriage of a hobo. He had a long orange coat, a round, baleful face covered in great tufts of fur like a mustache, and hurt eyes. He reminded me of the local drunk we saw most days, pushing his bike around town—old and broken-looking, but not ashamed. Joe crouched down to minister to Ricky, talking softly. The cat accepted the affection but kept its eyes level; you could tell he had gotten used to not expecting much. Joe turned and looked up at me with a funny, hurt look in his own eyes.

"What do you think? Do you like him?"

Did I like him? The question undid me. Maybe it was the sadness of the little animal, or Joe's attraction to that sadness. Maybe it was how shabby the place seemed, despite the volunteers and their sweet signs. Maybe it just was the idea that someone *wouldn't* like a cat like Ricky, and would say so.

"Yeah," I said, smiling, hoping I didn't also look like I was about to cry. "He looks like a great cat to me."

Getting a cat felt like a big deal to Joe, so he didn't take Ricky on the spot. A young guy in an old flannel shirt came in to clean the cages, and Joe, ever friendly, told him he thought he'd come back to adopt Ricky tomorrow. The next morning we drove over there together, having decided to take Ricky home, but when we got there the cat was gone.

"Oh, it looks like someone adopted him last night," the teenage girl at the desk said, frowning. The timing of it felt like more than a coincidence—my guess is that someone who worked at the shelter liked Ricky too, and when they found out that Joe was considering adopting him they beat him to it. It didn't matter; Joe found Georgia that day and brought her home instead, and he ended up loving that old sourpuss with his whole heart.

And about six months after all this, the shelter got shut down. Apparently it had been run so poorly that some of the animals were getting sick and malnourished, and an employee reported it anonymously. The director of the shelter, who was in her 80s, was arrested on several counts of animal cruelty and about a dozen cats had to be put down by the state SPCA. They took over the place temporarily, re-housing the surviving animals while they worked to get it up to code.

Joe and I were in his little kitchen—Georgia sitting on the floor between us, her fluffy tail flickering—when we read about the case on a local news website. I remembered the dingy building and the lonely animals and felt that same dirty sadness again as I thought about good intentions and the long, dark stretch of distance between wanting to do the right thing and actually doing it.

30

GEORGIA

O h, Georgia. What a great old gal.

Georgia was elderly when Joe met her. There was something so touching about her—I guess it was her age. She couldn't keep weight on easily so she felt delicate and frail. But she was comically bright and inquisitive, and she had a luxurious coat of long, grey fur.

Joe didn't name her Georgia—she already had the name when he adopted her, and the people at the shelter told us that her previous owner ran a luncheonette where the cat had lived. She loved sitting under Joe's kitchen table, and we couldn't sit there without her weaving through our legs and feet. We attributed her kitchen habits to her past as a cafe cat.

Joe was so kind to that cat, it sort of broke my heart to see it— except for when he laid it on too thick. He made up songs and crooned them to her as he carried her around in his arms, and sometimes used a baby voice. The baby voice was a bit much.

Joe liked to take Georgia outside whenever he could, which had a way of lighting her up afterward and making her even more sprightly. Once, the two of them met me at a train station in the suburbs as a surprise. When I got off the train I looked around for Joe—*him* I was expecting—and was startled to see them sitting together on a patch of grass across the street. She was so mild-mannered that he didn't need a leash for her; she stuck close to him while he stroked her fur. People kept walking by and doing double-takes: "Is that a cat?"

I lived with Georgia for a year or so, after I moved out to the boonies to join Joe. I didn't enjoy being there too much—it was my one and only experience with living in the country and I found it really boring and kind of spooky—but Georgia and I made a solid friendship that year. I spent a lot of time curled up in my papasan chair—you know, those big round ones that you tuck yourself into, like a bird in a nest—and she liked to join me there. She was so tiny that she'd hop up onto my lap and I'd hardly feel it. After she got comfortable, she'd move the tip of her bushy tail in contentment, like flicking a feather duster.

For such a diminutive cat, she had a huge attitude, though. Somehow she was able to make her footsteps quite loud as she stomped through the apartment. We called her the Clydesdale because she had a habit of walking rather formally and picking her feet up high off the ground, like a show horse. That, and she had long fur on her legs that hung down over her feet.

We didn't get to bring Georgia with us when we moved back to Philadelphia. She died about a month before we left, after losing a lot of weight over just a few weeks. I have never seen Joe so sad, before or since. There's something special about having a pet that's just your own, and as much as I loved her, those two had a friendship that was unique to them alone.

31

COCO

Coco's body spreads out when she lies down somewhere and she melts into a puddle of cat. A pudgy, fuzzy puddle made of velvet. She's a "Siamese mix," her adoption paper says, though we don't know what she's mixed with, or anything else about her, because we got her at the pound. She has the coloring of a Siamese—the dark brown mask on the face, dark brown ears, and dark brown feet and belly—but a round face and adorable cobby build. This cat is unusually beautiful. Her coat has all the colors of a roasted marshmallow, and also those of a loaf of marble pound cake. Her fur is velour-short on her feet: Rich, brown devil's-food-cake feet. Cinnamon, nutmeg, brown sugar, molasses cat. She has bright blue eyes that look lavender when she gazes up into the full natural light coming through the window. Elizabeth Taylor, eat your heart out.

I'm in love again, dammit. After Trixie I thought I'd never love another cat. After Georgia, Joe thought he never would either. But one day, after we'd been in our new house for a few months, I guess he felt ready. He texted me from the pet store where he was buying stuff for our fish.

"I'M AT THE PET STORE AND I HAVE SOMETHING TO TELL YOU."

We went back there together later that day and I agreed that the cat he'd fallen for was wonderful. The sign said she was 13 years old, which gave me a sharp twinge in my solar plexus when I read it. Georgia was around that age when Joe adopted her, and she only lived for another two years after that. But you know what? We can take it. There's no love without loss, and in the midst of life we are in death, *etcetera*.

The cat was already named Coco when we adopted her and we liked the name, though it would have felt wrong to change it even if we didn't. That said, we usually call her Bobo instead. She's inherently ridiculous, so it suits her better. Like when she teeters on her cobby legs on the footrest of our recliner, playing seesaw with whoever's sitting in the chair. Such a Bobo.

Coco spends the night in her own bed downstairs, but lately she's taken to tucking us in first. Once we've turned out the lights and are in bed talking, we'll hear her trundle up the stairs. Recently we found this planetarium at the thrift store, a small battery-powered light with a plastic cut-out of the constellations on top, so that's part of our nightly routine now too: We turn off the lights and switch on the planetarium and watch a spray of stars splash across the ceiling. It's really romantic, like falling asleep on a rooftop or the deck of a ship. Coco sometimes likes to investigate the planetarium on the floor. She presses her nose against the light bulb, which turns the starry night overhead into a stormy night—a cloud passing across the sky. After that she'll climb onto Joe's chest and purr like a motor while he strokes her head, and after a few minutes of this she gets up and leaves, her job done.

Dark brown and sleek, with slits for eyes when she's feeling contented, Coco sometimes reminds me of a sea lion pup. The fur around her face is thick and rich looking, like she's wearing a mink stole and she *is* the mink stole at the same time. I could describe this cat's beauty for hours, pages. I think instead I'll write her a love poem. I'd planned to write a sonnet, but my dear friend Amanda Laughtland—an animal lover and a very good poet—reminded me that odes make great love poems too. So here you are, an Ode to Coco, the most beautiful critter that lives in my house.

An Ode to Coco

Your coloring's like a sugary treat, so sweet:
cinnamon belly, chocolate feet.
As fancy as you are delicious,
you prefer salmon to other fishes.
Sitting in the kitchen, snoozing on the floor—
you'll curl up on my lap, but you like Joe's more.
You chase your laser toy like a seasoned tennis champ—
darting and crouching, nearly breaking the lamp—
cuz for an elder cat you're really pretty zippy.
Never scratchy, occasionally nippy.
And just as often you like to sit and preen,
licking your coat of track-suit velveteen.

32

THE WHITE
WITCH'S CAT

And also: There's a cat who lives there. She's white, which has always struck me as a kind of sight gag, a reassuring comment on the type of witchcraft that's practiced there. She's entirely white with pea-green eyes and she looks ancient. She curls up and falls asleep everywhere, on top of everything, including the folded-up dragon t-shirts that I would like to buy if they weren't all covered in cat hair. On the store's website—which is also ancient—there's a newspaper article about the shop that was published in 1999. I read it just now and was stunned to see a picture of a white cat looking bright-eyed and slender. The caption says her name is Morgana. The hideous 90s layout of the website—you have to scroll and scroll and *scroll*—makes the story and the cat herself appear lodged in some long-ago time, but I would bet my life it's the same one I've seen there over the years. I've seen her as recently as six months ago, in fact. She must be twenty years old by now.

I guess it's magic.

33

GRACIE

Gracie's pretty cool. She's my mom's Valentine.

My mother got the cat from the pet store, where Animal Control does its adoptions. They were doing a Valentine's Day special all weekend: $14 to adopt any cat. She chose Gracie from a bunch of older kittens that were hopping around their cages, all of them calicos with patches of color over their white bellies and backs like they'd been *decoupaged*.

Gracie was hyper then, with a distinctly loony look in her eyes, and she is hyper now. You can't knit in her presence without her attacking your hands, and if you sit in the armchair in my mother's living room for any length of time she will eventually pop up beside you, scare the daylights out of you, and take a swipe at you with her claws. And my mom will laugh.

One time I dressed as Gracie. I guess I was inspired by her pretty coloring, watercolor greys and whites and tans all melting into each other. I'd promised my mother I'd go with her to some dinner at her church and I wanted to look nice, so I put on a soft, beige top and these tan, flat-front pants I wear when I'm trying to look grown-up, and I borrowed my mom's swishy grey cardigan to go over it. On our way to the front door we passed Gracie, who was rolling around on a throw rug my mom keeps there, acting crazy.

"Look, Mom." I said, laughing. "I look like the cat!"

It's possible I'd overidentified with Gracie, or felt a weird sort of sibling rivalry with her, since my mom was so infatuated with the cat and I knew she'd taken to sleeping in my old room, like a replacement child.

But I don't want to read too much into it.

34

POLLY & ONYX & BORIS

A few years ago, my sister's boyfriend had something of a stray cat problem at his mother's house. A litter of five kittens was born under a shed back there, so Liz and Marty—already experienced at trap-and-release programs—caught all of them in a humane trap, one at a time. It was quite the saga. Stray cats are hard to catch, and they never did get the mother. But after a few weeks of trying, they captured all five of the beautiful kittens: Two black ones and two grey tabbies and one that was completely grey, like a seal.

Liz was able to give two of the kittens away to a man who runs an organic vegetable farm. He planned to keep them as barn cats. But after a week she discovered the remaining three had ringworm, which meant the barn cats probably did too. She apologized profusely to the farmer—I always picture an old man in denim overalls, but Liz said he was in his thirties, a regular guy—and she had to go back to the farm to laboriously catch them in traps *again*. Then she brought all five of them to be quarantined in our mother's garage until they were better and no longer contagious.

I saw the litter once, when I was at my mom's house for a visit. Liz was due to stop by to feed them and give them their medicine, as she did twice a day. When she got there I followed her into the dark, underused garage—it feels like a root cellar in there, but on this occasion it was bright with the energy of five small but enthusiastic lives. The kittens were hopping around and falling over each other in their cardboard box. They really were awfully cute, fungal infection and patchy fur notwithstanding. I wasn't allowed to touch them because of the ringworm, so I just looked at them and smiled, and one of the black ones—I think it was Onyx—sat there calmly looking back at me.

Liz pulled the box out onto the lawn to clean it and let the cats play, and after a while I went back into the kitchen where my mom and I stood looking out the window at my sister tending to these cats. She knelt on one knee in the grass and her light blonde hair glowed yellow in the sunlight, a dusty halo around her head. She seemed to radiate a certain melancholy, too, like our dad always did. It's an aura that's often there, I think, but I can only see it when she doesn't know I'm looking, like when she's driving the car and I sneak a look at the side of her face. That's what I remember when I think of those cats; Liz's dusty sadness aura, which actually looked very pretty and peaceful in the afternoon sun.

Eventually the barn cats went back to the vegetable farm, but the other three remain in Liz's life. Marty's mother took Polly, the only female of the litter. Marty has Boris, a beautiful Russian Blue with velvety grey fur and high-set, almond-shaped eyes. And Liz took Onyx, one of the black ones. He's all grown now, but he's still as shy and wily as when he was an almost-forgotten stray in a cardboard box.

35

BAD BAD & FARFEL

I hate New York. It's impossible there. You barely get to actually experience it when you're there; you just get swept up in the tide of humanity that never stops moving.

But I mean, I love it there, too. It's complicated.

When I was growing up in Philadelphia in the 80s, nearby New York loomed large over us. It was still scary then. Scary, but interesting. Weirdos moved there from small towns all over America, looking for a place where they could be weird freely. You could be a broke artist there, get lost in the crowd and find yourself a few years later, totally changed. These days the city belongs to rich people, and the graffiti that once covered the subway cars like flamboyant, hot-pink wallpaper has all been washed away.

Everyone knows all this already; pretentious fools like me love to crow about how sanitized New York is now. I know that. But I'm telling you, it's not the same place it once was. You have to have so much money to do anything at all there, but somehow everywhere you look it's nothing but Starbucks and Forever 21s, like a giant mall. It's depressing.

Anyhow, a few summers ago I spent a week on the Lower East Side to look after my friend's cats while she was away. She had neighbors in the building who could feed the cats for her, of course, but she thought I might like the excuse to stay in New

York for a few days for free. And I did, because I always forget that I hate New York.

This friend of mine is very devoted to her cats. Their names are Bad Bad (Leroy Brown) and Farfel, and they take up happy residence in her cluttered, cozy pad. Like my friend, the cats were easy-going and low-maintenance. There was only one rule: Close the bathroom door when you're not in there (or when you are) or Farfel will stand on his hind legs and tear all the toilet paper off the roll.

I had some fun that week, but I felt really lonely. I don't even know why. I met a friend who took me to the High Line Park, which was cool: A long, narrow garden of wildflowers planted on a disused railway, thirty feet above the streets of Chelsea. I finally made the trip out to the Cloisters, too, an art museum in upper Manhattan that's constructed partially out of pieces of French abbeys and fortified like a real medieval building. Like a castle! One ride on the J train and a transfer to the A and an hour later I was in Europe, in the countryside, in the middle ages. I could see the cliffs of the Palisades across the river, and the trees above them, and nothing else, even though I was still standing in Manhattan. It was so jarring it was almost transcendent, the kind of experience you can only have in New York.

But I wasn't exactly enjoying myself. On my way back from the Cloisters, someone screamed something unintelligible at me from his car. Later, some lady shoved me through the doorway of a bodega because I wasn't moving fast enough. I got a gross cold at some point and couldn't sleep at night, so I lay there and watched the light and shadow from passing cars move and grow across the ceiling, feeling my stomach start to ache the way it always does when I've been awake too long. I remember this now and say to myself, "Why the hell didn't you just turn on the light and read a book, or play some music? Smoke some cigarettes and go for a walk? You were in New York City. There's so much to see!" But I can't explain myself to myself. I just couldn't find a way to feel happy.

The cats were good company, though. Bad Bad was a charmer, but Farfel, with his wiry body and grey stripes, was a real hoot. I only forgot to close the bathroom door once, when I left the apartment to get some food. When I got back, I found him lying on the enormous nest of shredded toilet paper he'd made on the middle of the bed, totally unapologetic as only a cat can be. It cheered me right up. The mess was easy to clean but I took a picture first, to send to my friend. I guessed that she wouldn't be mad about the waste, and I was right. She was in Chile for a wedding, which had been held the night before on top of a dormant volcano. A more picturesque scene I couldn't imagine, but she wasn't having any fun either. The elevation made her dizzy, she said, and she missed her cats.

36

CHICKEN LIVERS

I've heard so many stories about Chicken Livers. I even met him once, I mean as much as anyone can meet a cat like that. Someone opened the back door and he went streaking across the lawn where we were having a cocktail party, nothing but light and movement, and we all hopped out of his way. Chicken Livers has a reputation, you see.

The cat belonged to Hugo, the unbelievably eccentric man who owned the company Joe worked for while he was still in college. I can't give you too much detail about him because he comes from a famous family that would be very easily identified, but suffice it to say he was the son of one the richest men in the world and had lived the sort of life you'd imagine such a person living—before he became estranged from his family of origin, that is, and settled in suburban New Jersey, where he ran a small business and ate take-out Chinese. Improbable, but true. Hugo had lived in Abu Dhabi; he knew David Bowie. His mother was a model and so was one of his sisters, and he'd had three wives. A really famous guitarist—whom I also shouldn't name—once offered to pay him for a night with one of his beautiful female friends. (Hugo declined.) And though his fortunes had changed considerably since those high-flying times, Hugo still had a presence that filled the room, and green eyes that gleamed with intelligence and a few lifetimes' worth of stories.

Like his larger-than-life owner, Chicken Livers was a force to be reckoned with. He could not be contained and regularly escaped the house to go carousing in the neighborhood. He also liked to go on walks with Hugo. Every evening the two of them would roam all over town and come back in time for dinner. On one of these outings, Chicken Livers viciously attacked someone's dog—yes, *dog*—who was so badly hurt that the owners called for the cat to be put down. Hugo couldn't bear the thought of losing his friend, so instead he put Chicken Livers under house arrest for several months, and made the cat's incarceration more comfortable by building him a special enclosure in an upstairs window. Chicken Livers spent that summer more or less happily, sitting in his cat-sized window box, sniffing the air through the screen and dreaming of the time when he would be allowed to go back out and raise some more hell.

37

MORE
BOOKSTORE
CATS

Have you ever been to Jim Thorpe, Pennsylvania? It's such a weird place. A tiny, Victorian town cut into the side of a mountain; it's really only got one street, which winds back and back and back. Most of what surrounds it is state park and game lands; nothing but mountains and trees. When we were there for a weekend visit, Joe and I stayed in an old inn that had upstairs porches like the ones in New Orleans. On Saturday night, the street out front blossomed into a roughneck party scene as people from all over the county drove in to drink at the bar next door, then start loud arguments and gun their engines. There was a burlesque show in town that weekend, too. They performed at the opera house, a restored vaudeville theater with lights over the sign out front that glowed yellow in the August night, and chain smokers with rocker hair hung around the entrance waiting for the show to start. Ladies in corsets strolled the streets all weekend, like visiting dignitaries. There were a lot of tattoos.

Joe and I didn't get drunk or go to the strip tease. Instead we roamed around, aimless in the summer heat, exploring the town like two kids with nothing to do. We talked to the ukulele-playing hippie girl who worked at the coffee shop one morning, and then we drove to a park and went swimming in the glacier-clean lake. It was me and him and dozens of little kids, all of us bobbing up and down and laughing. When we got back to town, we saw there was a book sale at the library. I bought a collection of ghost stories and Joe got a DVD called "Learn to Play the Ukulele" for twenty-five cents. We walked back over to the coffee shop to give it to our new friend, who was out front, about to climb onto her bike and ride away.

"Hey, ukulele girl!" I called after her, going briefly blind with shyness. "We got you something!"

We found other books that weekend, too. Before the trip, I'd researched the town and found a used bookstore I wanted to visit, and it didn't disappoint. Practically the moment we walked in, once my eyes had adjusted to the dim light, I saw a book of Nuala O'Faolain's essays for the *Irish Times*. Talk about a treat. O'Faolain is one of my all-time favorites, but I didn't even know this book existed. I sat down on the floor with it, ready to dig in.

A large cat sauntered over and curled up next to me on the floor. *Yes.* I was hoping this would happen. I'd seen the cat when we walked in, but in my experience, you get more cat attention by playing it cool than by acting eager. I'd ignored her and was victorious. The cat had a tortoiseshell back and a vast white belly, which she showed me by turning over onto her side. She seemed to go to sleep the moment she got comfortable, but when I stood up to go to another part of the shop she jumped up and followed me. A prim girl who was stocking shelves nearby said, without seeming to look over, "Her name is Zoe. She's friendly." And she certainly was. Everywhere I went Zoe followed me, and each time she hoisted herself back to her feet she did it a bit begrudgingly, as if it was her job.

Eventually Joe and I went up to pay for our books, and behind the battered wooden counter was another cat, sleeping on a chair. It was a black cat that had draped itself across the chair's back, and I didn't realize it wasn't the girl's sweater until Joe asked her if the other cat was friendly, too.

38

FARKLE

I never knew Farkle, but Joe did. He belonged to Joe's dad's parents, in their house in Piscataway, New Jersey. Joe says Farkle was mean, but it sounds like he was just annoying.

Every morning, Farkle woke Joe's grandparents up by standing in the bedroom door and yowling. His grandfather had to get out of bed and go downstairs to let the cat out into the backyard— it was their morning routine. But all Farkle wanted to do was walk around to the front of the house, where he'd immediately demand to be let back in. That gave his grandfather just enough time to get back into bed and warm up again before the cat started throttling the storm door, clinging to the screen with its claws and using its body weight to bang the door in its frame. The noise was too loud to ignore, so he had to get up again to let the cat in, and he'd stay up that time, bringing in the paper and putting on the coffee.

I never knew Joe's dad's father, but his presence haunts the air, a bit like my own grandfather's always did. I never knew that man either. From the sound of it, his grandpop was an old-fashioned man's man; stoic and dependable. I laugh along with the rest of the family when Joe reminisces about what a pain Farkle was and imitates his owner's irritated cussing into the cold morning air.

39

OLIVIA

y mother and sister both volunteer for Animal Control in Philadelphia, looking after the cats and helping to adopt them out from pet stores around the city. As you can probably imagine, Animal Control in a city like this one is pretty taxed. Something like thirty percent of the *people* who live here are struggling below the poverty line, so animals are an afterthought, and these mangy little scroungers on the street don't get a lot of support.

The pet store program is good, though. Every few days a volunteer from Animal Control's main branch brings a new batch of cats to the store where my mom helps out and they take up residence there for a while, living in cages with blankets and toys for company. Almost all of them get adopted within a week or two and the kittens go even faster. My mother goes in a few times a week to feed the cats and clean their boxes—whatever needs doing—so she gets to know them during the short time they live in the store.

"Some of the cats are so *bad*," she told me recently. I always get the update. Recently the bad one was Jimmy, a great big white cat who was tireless in his attempts to escape his enclosure while he was being fed and cleaned up. I can picture my mom trying to hold onto this big galoot while he thrashed his tail around, her glasses and hair all askew. She is no wimp, but at sixty-eight, or however old she is now, she can look a bit taken aback by this sort of thing.

After Sylvia, my mother's queenly Persian cat, died, her house felt too quiet. She kept her eye on the cats that came to the store for adoption, and soon she met a kitten named Leonard. (Who names these cats?) He was tiny, just a few months old, and had a sweet personality. The adoptions are handled by a different volunteer, so my mother went in on one of her off days to see about bringing little Leonard home. But when she arrived, a man was already there with his young son, hoping to adopt him. The little boy was, in point of fact, *dying* to adopt Leonard. At one point he was so overcome with emotion that he sat down on the floor and sort of tipped over sideways with longing, saying something about *"the kittennnn."* So my sainted mother stepped back and let them take Leonard home.

Luckily there is never a shortage of cats at Animal Control. My mom got to know Olivia for a week or two before she was taken in by the cat's antics and decided to take her instead. Olivia is tall, with long legs and a pert posture. She goes tip-toeing around on her long legs with her tail sticking straight up, alert to anything she might sense in the air, like a weathervane. She's a blithe spirit and a giant pest, standing on my mother's lap and staring her right in her face. Her loony attitude makes Gracie seem downright mature in comparison. The two cats both get along with humans very nicely, but they occasionally try to murder each other, so my mom keeps them separated by doors and toddler gates. She dreams of the day when the three of them—my mother and her two cats—can live harmoniously, each one curled up on a separate cushion and watching TV.

40

PET SHOP KITTEN PARTY

I hate Christmas but I enjoy the idea of it, strolling around and looking at people's decorations and stuff. One year for Christmas, Joe and I went away for the weekend. Not *over* Christmas, mind you, which would have been a dream—I do, I *dream* of the day that I can go away and not let Christmas happen to me—but earlier in the month, for a holiday getaway.

We spent a lovely weekend in a small town outside the city, drinking coffee and holding hands. We ran out of things to do after the first day, so on the second day we visited the town's small pet shop for entertainment. Maybe they'd have exotic birds or something, we thought. Even better: They had cats. A ton of them! And to our delight, most of them were kittens. We cooed and put our fingers through the bars of their cages, trying to touch their fuzzy bodies. A lanky, soft-spoken guy with long hair came over.

"You guys can play with them, if you want. We let them out every morning anyway to get some exercise. I'll do it now," he said. And with that, he started flicking open cages, and before you knew it there were cats everywhere, maybe twelve of them in this small shop, rolling around on the floor and hopping up onto shelves, each of them mewing to try to steal our attention away from the others. All of them but one.

One of the kittens was white and tiny and very timid. The others had been dying to get out of their cages all along, but this one didn't seem to want to lose the security of being locked in. Once the door was open, it looked even more afraid, and cowered in a back corner. I made a sad face at the long-haired metal dude and he was like, "Yeah, that one likes to be left alone." His voice was a low murmur, the hallmark of a shy young man. Then he turned and slipped into some stockroom in the back.

So I did; I left the cat alone. I played it cool, examining a dog toy that looked like a hamburger, but it felt important that the quiet one should enjoy its freedom too, so I kept looking back to see what it was doing. Finally, when I turned to look, I saw that it had left its cage and was carefully picking its way across the tiled floor, all by itself. I had two pink hearts for eyes. Go get it, buddy! When I saw the metal dude come out from the back, I was excited to tell him about the white kitten.

"The little shy one came out of hiding!" I shouted as he walked past, and instead of answering me he ducked his head in what looked like extreme embarrassment, then disappeared down an aisle.

Oh my god, he thought I meant him. He thought I was calling him "the little shy one" and announcing his return from the back room to all the world, which of course would be enough to make a shy person feel like crawling into a hole and hiding there forever. Whoops. Sorry, shy metal dude. It was cool of you to let us play with the kittens. And it's still a nice memory, all these years later.

Joe and I went on a reading tour this summer, half vacation and half work. We packed up our hatchback and left Philly in August, heading for points north in the hope of escaping a heat wave that only ended up following us, first to Woodstock and then to Boston, where we went to an afternoon cook-out at a punk show space and stood there broiling on the parking lot blacktop. I tried to be polite while I drank their cheap beer, but you know how sometimes it just feels impossible to fake it? I'd had it with blinding city summers, the sun radiating off of every wall and sidewalk, air conditioners dripping stank water drops on my head from above. In the morning we would leave Boston for Rhode Island, where we'd stay on a farm that had goats and a pond you could swim in. It was all I could think about.

To get there, we drove down the blue-white coast of Massachusetts, then over long, low bridges into Rhode Island (state motto: "Hope"). We had to drive through the woods for a while to get to the goat farm, and the heat broke late that morning, finally, blessedly, so the air felt soft and mild. It was a windows-down, feet-on-the-dashboard kind of drive, the kind that always makes me imagine I could just keep going and leave my real life behind, become someone new.

The owner of the farm was a man named Adam, who, along with his partner, operated a small bed and breakfast on the property in an old barn they'd refurbished. When we arrived there, Joe pulled up next to the building that looked the most like a barn to us and we got out and stretched. The goats, maybe twenty of them, were nearby in their pen, staring at us with comical straightforwardness, and a smaller creature was toddling her way over to our car. It was a tiny, grey cat with black, paintbrush stripes, and she had a funny piece of felt hanging down from her collar, like a bib, which seemed to be the thing that made her toddle. Just a little though. She was clearly a tiny hellion who would not be slowed down by a bib or anything else.

A young guy came out of the farmhouse then, too, and walked up to us with one hand raised, smiling. Adam had overgrown blond hair and a few blurry blue tattoos and I liked him right away because he wasn't in a hurry and he looked like he never was.

"That's Petra," he said as the striped cat pressed her body against my legs.

"What's with the bib?" I asked him.

He told us the farm was situated next to a property that used to be a bird sanctuary and lots of birds still came around. Petra was the resident birder and the bib was designed to keep her from killing them all. She still got one sometimes, but the thing made her clumsy and gave the bird a chance to get away. When I squatted down to pet her, the bib was all wet from where she'd dragged it over the grass.

As the three of us talked, an orange tabby cat came sauntering up behind Adam. My face must have changed because he turned to look.

"Oh, that's Philip. He's kind of a doofus," he said. Philip had lived at the farm before Adam bought it, and since his old owner had passed away, Adam kept him. Before I had a chance to ask what was doofy about this graceful looking cat, Adam blurted, "We have another cat too, an older one. People have been asking if something's wrong with him, and—he's dying." I could see it pained him to say it, but he was trying to be polite so his voice came out stolid and thick. "The vet said that we won't have to euthanize him because he doesn't have any teeth left and he hasn't been interested in his food, so he'll just die."

It felt bad to hear that, I can't lie; I felt it in my stomach. But it sounded natural and right in a way, too; the kind of thing you'd expect a farmer to be able to say.

Joe and I didn't have a reading that night, so we had nothing to get ready for, nothing to do at all, so that's what we did: Nothing, just like the cats. We sat in the prickly grass and Petra and Philip did too. They climbed into our laps and tumbled over each other while making little rumbling sounds in their chests, and Petra hunted insects in the weeds that only she could see. I read a piece of travel writing recently in which the writer said that joy is found whenever you are totally enveloped in something. For a few hours, Joe and I were totally enveloped in the life of this farm. We climbed into the two plastic kayaks Adam said we could use and took them around the small pond, paddling quietly, looking for blueberry bushes (we found some bushes, but the berries were all gone). The cats waited patiently on the shore for us to return. When we kicked through the grass on our way back to the house, Petra chased us and Philip chased her.

If Petra was a huntress, Philip was just plain bad. While we tried to eat our dinner at a plastic picnic table that night, he twisted around in my lap and butted his head into my gut. He spent the rest of the evening napping on the hood of our car. That night, as we lay in bed in the dark—the thick, black, country dark; the kind I am not used to—we heard something bang down onto the low roof above us. It scared me, but then I remembered Adam telling us that Philip liked to climb trees and jump onto roofs. We still hadn't seen the third cat—his name was Muzzy—and before I fell asleep I remembered about him and wondered if he was okay.

•   •   •

When I woke up the next morning it seemed like it was raining, though I couldn't hear it. Joe wasn't in the bed next to me, so I got up and padded through the dim rooms. I found him standing at the back door, looking out the window. He pointed without saying anything: Sure enough, it was raining, and out on the cement porch, under a bench, a large but bony grey cat was curled up asleep. Muzzy. It had to be him. Joe opened the door quietly and we went over to him, squatted down. He was too skinny, so his head looked big and his eyes were huge and hungry and sad. He opened his mouth in greeting, but no sound came out, but he was beautiful and serene and he looked right at us, eyes glowing with a soft, grey-green light. He drank in the attention we gave him and preened as we stroked his head and back.

We spent the rest of that day with the cats too, just sort of coexisting with them. When the rain let up, we poked around in the woods behind the pond, and when it started up again I wanted to let the cats into the house with us, but they weren't allowed. Muzzy sat on the ground outside the sliding door and gazed in at us for a while before giving up and sloping away.

It's funny; the goats were the farm's big draw, of course, and they really were interesting and amusing to look at, all sneezy and snorty and inquisitive. There were twenty-four of them, as it happened, in various sizes and shades of pure white, pure black, and soft grey, and they tended to turn *en masse* and stare at every little thing we did when they weren't eating or pooping. But those cats, my goodness. We fell in love with them and I think it was mutual. By the end of that second day, the grass in front of the house was littered with curled-up mouse bodies, offerings to their new friends, the guests.

Before we left the next morning, we stood near our car and talked with Adam for a while, the way we had when we arrived.

He was wearing the same striped tank top as the day before. He told us some more about Muzzy, how he was his partner Ted's cat from when Ted was in college and sneaked the cat into his dorm room, a rescue who was probably nineteen years old by now. This time, Adam let himself look sad as he said it. While we were talking, Philip went streaking past us and dived into our car through the open driver's side door and we laughed about having a stowaway.

"We're a little annoyed with Philip right now," Adam said, frowning, "but he does seem to be mellowing out as he gets older."

Why were they annoyed with Philip, you ask? Because he likes to climb trees, as we've already seen, and very early one morning last summer he climbed all the way to the top of a 150-foot tree in a stand of beeches near the pond. Once he was up there he was too scared to come down and Adam, who is always up by four in the morning to start his work, heard him crying for help.

"A big storm was coming and I knew he would be killed up there. So I go out at 4:30 in the morning and take down the tree with a chainsaw and the cat's swaying around up at the top like crazy," he said, refusing to smile at the memory. Cutting down the tree could have killed the cat too, of course, but it had to be done. Adam had bought special climbing boots for the sole purpose of rescuing this doofus from other trees he'd gotten stuck in, but it would be foolish to go up that high. He brought the tree down as carefully as he could and let it crash gently into a clump of shorter trees nearby, and when the cat saw his chance he scrambled down and took off running for the shelter of the barn.

So we'd met three cats: The tranquil old guy who was about to die and seemed to know it; the tough little female whose killer instinct had to be curbed; and this one, the cat who'd been inherited, and who risked his life with his joyful, idiot sense of adventure. I think I learned something from them all.

42

THE BACKYARD SAGA GOES ON AND ON

Spring is finally here, and I for one could not be happier. I don't hate the cold weather like some people do, but it's always exciting to see everything come back to life. Yesterday I stood in my kitchen, bare feet on the tile, yellow sunlight filling the room, and I could hear birds singing for the first time in months. I had to hold still and listen hard to be sure of what I was hearing. It was so, so nice.

We didn't have a tough winter, but we did get one serious snowstorm; a bona fide blizzard. It came at the end of that bitter cold week I told you about, when we made a shelter out back for the strays. They talked about the storm all week before it started, and I felt badly worried about the cats, the one remaining kitten in particular. I've never lived in a house in the city before this, only in apartments, and the house I grew up in was in a suburb, where there were fewer stray cats. This has been my first experience seeing these animals up close. I was surprised to find that I feel responsible for them.

So Joe and I bought a Styrofoam cooler and cut a doorway into the side, then filled it with straw we got at a plant nursery. We didn't need much, just enough to keep the cats warm and dry on those vicious winter nights. I saw the Mama cat and the Bad Mammer Jammer come out of there one morning, so I know they used it at least once. But we never saw the baby again after that week. It disappeared just before the blizzard—they all did, the mother and father too, and I hoped they'd found a warm place to hide, maybe under someone's porch one street over where the houses are bigger. The two grown cats eventually started coming around again, looking for food, but the kitten is gone. I don't like thinking about it too much because I don't know what it means. The weather was dangerous for a while—they said on the news you could get frostbite in fifteen minutes if you weren't properly covered.

But you know, someone in the neighborhood might have found the kitten and taken it in. It's also possible that it was weaned by the time the weather turned cold and that it left its mother to go off on its own the way cats are naturally inclined to do. Maybe it's doing just fine, having joined the ranks of the other neighborhood cats, hunting for its food and living in freedom. I wonder if I'd recognize it if I saw it again, full-grown and in command of its powers, stretching and warming its body in a patch of dirty sun.

43

CAT'S CAT

Joe had a good friend in high school whose name was Cat. After they graduated, she moved around a lot, eventually ending up in Baltimore for a while. He went to visit her there once, in the squat she shared with some other artists in a disused warehouse. Cat had a cat, a distinguished old gentleman that she called Beauregard. One night, she did acid and she and the cat had a conversation that went on for hours. During their talk, Beauregard told Cat that his real name was Mister Sister. She felt deepened by this information, later remarking to Joe that she'd never before considered her foolishness in thinking she could know a cat's true name without asking.

SUBSCRIBE TO EVERYTHING WE PUBLISH!

Do you love what Microcosm publishes?

Do you want us to publish more great stuff?

Would you like to receive each new title as it's published?

Subscribe as a BFF to our new titles and we'll mail them all to you as they are released!

$10-30/mo, pay what you can afford. Include your t-shirt size and your birthday for a possible surprise!

microcosmpublishing.com/bff

...AND HELP US GROW YOUR SMALL WORLD!

More on Love, Animals, and Recovery: